ST. MICHAEL

St. Michael

John Michael Gurule

To order additional copies of this book, contact:
Xlibris
844-714-8691
www.Xlibris.com
Orders@Xlibris.com
823942

CONTENTS

John Michael Gurule

ST. MICHAEL
THE ARCHANGEL

Saint Michael the Archangel,
defend us in battle.
Be our protection against the
wickedness and snares
of the devil.
May God rebuke him,
we humbly pray,
O Prince of the heavenly hosts,
by the power of God,
thrust into hell
Satan and all evil spirits
who wander through the world
For the ruin of souls.
Amen

INTRODUCTION

BREAK
the chains of addiction

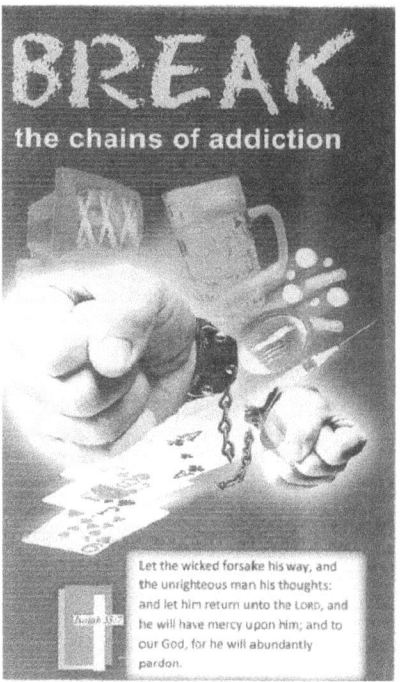

Isaiah 55:7

Let the wicked forsake their way, and sinners their thoughts; Let them turn to the Lord to find mercy; to our God, who is generous in forgiving.

I, John M Gurule, wanted to take the time to thank you, Fr. Warren Broussard S.J. Pastor, also Bishop Rogers, Selma Rogers, and Rachael Padilla for your angel testimony. I really appreciate your help.

CHAPTER 1

Autobiography

I, John Michael Gurule, admit that my problem was with alcohol and drugs. I started drinking and smoking weed at 15 years old. I did a few more things when I hit high school, like LSD, hard liquor, and beer. During that time in my life, I was working and going to school. By the time I turned 17 years old, I decided to join the army to avoid getting into trouble. I was doing well in the army until I ran into medical problems. Hiatal hernia is what I had; this occurs when the upper part of your stomach bulges through the large muscle separating your abdomen and chest. Your diaphragm has a small opening, hiatus, through which your food tube esophagus passes before connecting to your stomach. In a hiatal hernia, the stomach pushes up through that opening and into your chest. I was suffering a lot with chest pains. I was called into the lieutenant's office where I talked to two lieutenants and they asked me if I wanted to get out of the army. They said the doctor agreed to a medical discharge, and the lieutenants agreed to a honorable discharge, so I said yes. It wasn't until I got out of the army that I had x-rays of my chest, and I was told I would need to have surgery to repair the hiatal hernia. I have not gotten that surgery yet, still waiting. I did go back to work. I did start drinking alcohol again, and later in life harder drugs. I didn't understand why all my life I have worked but continued with a drug and alcohol problem. And sometimes I would get myself into problems. I would end up in treatment programs, Christian homes, jails, hospitals, and even prisons. I would eventually get out of these places feeling better and healthy. I felt I could conquer this addiction and resist the temptations and negative attitudes of alcohol and drugs. But pride would set in, and after a while I would fall apart again. I have been in over twenty different programs. Most of which are in the first book I wrote. "A Forty Year Journey with God in Albuquerque New Mexico." It seems to be the first half of my story. I know this because I entered what seemed to be my last recovery program here in Albuquerque, New Mexico. The V.A. Medical treatment center, a ninety-day program. I was still going through some life-changing stuff with my addiction. During that time I do remember going to a Catholic book store to look for a card about Michael The Archangel, I was going though some Satan and Demon attacks, so I decided I would need more help to stay clean and sober. So I buy the card and inside the card tells me a lot about who Michael The Archangel is. So I decided to write the second book about God, Jesus Christ, the Holy Spirit and Michael The Archangel, and the angels Gabriel and Raphael. These are angels you can find in the bible also and I will tell you about these Angels stories. In the bible there are many angels you can read about, there are thousands of these holy angels. This second book will be called Michael the Archangel, or who is like unto God? You will learn a lot about Michael the Archangel from this card. This book is an enlightening story about me who despite my weaknesses as a person, I never gave up and instead found hope to change my life with Jesus Christ, and the church of God. With this book, I'm sharing an open testimony and declaration of faith and an Oath to stay clean and sober and faithfulness to the Lord. Publication date June 13, 2013 of first book. "A Forty Year Journey with God in Albuquerque New Mexico."

This second book is about fighting off evil in my life, praying for others and about Michael the Archangel, because he also fights evil for anyone who truly wants to change.

Chapter 1

So, you can change your life around, and give your life to Jesus Christ you can, he is your Savior.

In John 3:16, For God so loved the world that he gave his only Son, so that everyone who believes in him might not perish but might have eternal life.

The bible says there is only one way to heaven.

Act 3:19, Repent, therefore, and be converted, that your sins may be wiped away.

Are you ready to accept God's gift of salvation by repenting of your sins and surrendering your life to the Lord Jesus Christ?

In John 14:6, Jesus said to him, "I am the way and the truth and the life. No one comes to the Father except through me."

Before I get started on the Michael the Archangel story, and the stories of Gabriel and Raphael, both angels from heaven, let me share with you about salvation.

In the bible, both Jesus Christ and John the Baptist preached repentance and salvation.

The gift of salvation is only attained by faith in Jesus Christ. Pray and ask Jesus to come into your heart and save you today. In Romans 10:13, For everyone who calls on the name of the Lord will be saved.

What does it mean to repent biblically?

The definition of Repentance, called for throughout the bible, is a summons to a personal, absolute and ultimate unconditional surrender to God as Sovereign. Though it includes sorrow or regret, it is more than that... In repenting one makes a complete change of one's direction (180° turn) toward God.

So where will you spend eternity?

God's word says that after you die you will be judged and go to heaven or hell.

Hebrews 9:27, Just as it is appointed that human beings die once, and after this the judgment.

Matthew 13:49, 50, Thus it will be at the end of the age. The angels will go out and separate the wicked from the righteous and throw them into the fiery furnace, where there will be wailing and grinding of teeth.

When asked, most people think they are going to heaven because they're not that bad, or because they are religious. I considered myself to be religious until I learned I was on my way to hell because I was living a lukewarm life. Here are some scriptures for people living a lukewarm life.

Revelation 3:15, 16, - I know your works; I know that you are neither cold nor hot. I wish you were either cold or hot. So, because you are lukewarm, neither hot nor cold, I will spit you out of my mouth.

Titus 1:16, They claim to know God, but by their deeds they deny him. They are vile and disobedient and unqualified for any good deed.

Matthew 7:21, 23, "Not everyone who says to me, 'Lord, Lord', will enter the kingdom of heaven," but only the one who does the will of my Father in heaven. Many will say to me on that day, 'Lord, Lord, did we not prophesy in your name? Did we not drive out demons in your name? Did we not do mighty deeds in your name? Then I will declare to them solemnly, 'I never knew you. Depart from me, you evildoers.

The bible teaches that we are all sinners and all guilty of breaking God's commandments.

Romans 5:8, But God proves his love for us in that while we were still sinners Christ died for us.

Romans 3:23, all have sinned, and are deprived of the glory of God.

Romans 6:23, for the wages of sin is death, but the gift of God is eternal life in Jesus Christ our Lord.

The gift of salvation is only attained by faith in Jesus Christ, not any of our religion or works. We will never be good enough to earn our way into heaven.

Titus 3:5, not because of any righteous deeds we had done.

Faith means putting our trust into Jesus Christ alone for our salvation, not our good works, not a church or its rituals, not saints or any other man-made traditions.

1 Timothy 2:5, For there is one God. There is also one mediator between God and the human race, Christ Jesus, himself human.

Acts 4:12, There is no salvation through anyone else, nor is there any other name under heaven given to the human race by which we are to be saved.

Romans 10:9, 10, For if you confess with your mouth that Jesus is Lord and believe in your heart that God raised him from the dead, you will be saved. For one believes with the heart and so is justified, and one confesses with the mouth and so is saved.

John 1:12, But to those who did accept him he gave power to become children of God, to those who believe in his name.

Ephesians 3:17, 18, and that Christ may dwell in your hearts by hearts through faith; that you, rooted and grounded in love, may have strength to comprehend with all the holy ones what is the breadth and length and height and depth, and to know the love of Christ that surpasses knowledge, so that you may be filled with all the fullness of God.

Roman's 10:13, No trial has come to you but what is human. God is faithful and will not let you be tried beyond your strength; but with the trial he will also provide a way out, so that you may be able to bear it.

Pray and ask Jesus Christ to come into your heart and save you today, Amen.

So as I read all these scriptures, I was ready to surrender my life to God and I did what the book of Romans 10:9, 13 said, For, if you confess with your mouth that Jesus is Lord and believe in your heart that God raised him from the dead, you will be saved. For one believes with the heart and so is justified, and one confesses with the mouth and so is saved. For the scripture says, no one who believes in him will be put to shame. For there is no distinction between Jew and Greek; the same Lord is Lord of all, enriching all who call upon him.

So, I prayed all these prayers and asked Jesus Christ, God Almighty, and the Holy Spirit into my life, and to save me from these medications I was on.

I was still on medication that was hard to get off of so, on August 22, 2017, I entered Vocational Rehabilitation at the V.A. Medical Center. I was there about eighty-five days and I was released on November 17, 2017. I am now medication free. I was very happy about my situation and I was going to stay free from any addictions. For while I was there I realized two things, how I got here and what I was going to do next.

Number one, I paid $,2,000.00 for a book I wrote and was published by Xlibris. The book is entitled, "A Forty Year Journey with God in Albuquerque New Mexico." Then I also gave $4,000.00 to a local church of God. A total of $6,000.00. That was my number one intention in that I wanted to share my story with others that may be in a similar situation, and also to give to a church of God that ministers to God.

In Malachi 3:6, 12, For, I, the Lord do not change, and you, son of Jacob, do not cease to be. Since the days of your ancestors you have turned aside from my statutes and have not kept them. Return to me, that I may return to you, says the Lord of hosts. But you say, "Why should we return?" Can anyone rob God? But you are robbing me? And you say, "How have we robbed you?" Of tithes and contributions! You are indeed accursed, for you, the whole nation, rob me. Bring the whole tithe into the storehouse, that there may be food in my house. Put me to the test, says the Lord of hosts, and see if I do not open the floodgates of heaven for you, and pour down upon you blessing without measure! I will rebuke the locust for you so that it will not destroy your crops, and the vine in the field will not be barren, says the Lord of hosts. All the nations will call you blessed, for you will be a delightful land, says the Lord of hosts.

Ok, number two realization: I was going to write a second book which is the second half of my story in this journey of mine. In the introduction of this book, I buy a card with an illustration of Michael the Archangel defeating a demon with wings. Inside the card are all the stories you will find in the bible which are true. So, I bought this card in a Catholic book store, because I was going through struggles (felt I was being attacked by the evil one) and I knew I was going to need more help to stay clean and sober. Inside the card told me a lot about who Michael the Archangel is. I found out he is the Captain of the armies of God, the type of divine fortitude, the champion of every faithful soul in strife with the powers of evil. Michael, or "who is like unto God.

In this second book, you'll learn more about God Almighty, Jesus Christ, and the Holy Spirit. The story of Michael the Archangel, and also two more angels, Gabriel, and Raphael. You will also see on the front of this card, St Michael is often depicted wielding a sword and a set of scales to vanquish Satan. His scales have an ancient and surprising meaning. The definition of the word vanquish is to conquer, to defeat triumph over, be victorious over the devil. Amen. So, the second realization is to write the second half of my story of how I was able to stay clean and sober.

Starting with the stories of Michael the Archangel, you will read about Michael in the bible five times. I will give the scriptures, and part of the story.

Then we will go through the St. Michael card, we will learn all the stories, and St. Michael's prayer.

Top 5 Bible Verses About Michael The Archangel:
1) Daniel 10:13-14, "but the prince of the kingdom of Persia stood in my way for twenty-one days, until finally Michael, one of the chief princes, came to help me. I left him there with the prince of the kingdom of Persia and came to make you understand what shall happen to your people in the last days; for there is yet a vision concerning those days."

2) Daniel 10:21, "but I shall tell you what is written in the book of truth. No one supports me against these except Michael, your prince.

3) Daniel 12:1, "At that time shall arise Michael, the great prince, guardian of your people; it shall be a time unsurpassed in distress since the nation began until that time. At that time your people shall escape, everyone who is found written in the book."

4) Jude 1:9, Yet the archangel Michael, when he argued with the devil in a dispute over the body of Moses, did not venture to pronounce a reviling judgment upon him but said, "May the Lord rebuke you!"

5) Revelation 12:7-8, Then war broke out in heaven; Michael and his angels battled against the dragon. The dragon and its angels fought back but they did not prevail and there was no longer any place for them in heaven.

So, this is my second realization in that I need to write the second half of my story of the Holy of Holies, and St. Michael The Archangel prayer. This is what I needed to fight off these Satan and demon attacks.

St. Michael the Archangel, defend us in battle. Be our protection against the wickedness and snares of the devil. May God rebuke him, we humbly pray, O Prince of the heavenly hosts, by the power of God, thrust into hell Satan and all evil spirits who wander through the world for the ruin of souls. Amen.

My eighty-five days in the very last program was over in the V.A. medical treatment center. I came out healthy and strong again and I'm thinking I have conquered my addiction. It wasn't even a week, and I relapsed back to drugs and alcohol. Two weeks go by and my doctor calls me in for a follow-up visit. I gave a blood test and a urinalysis. Well, I came out not so good and the doctor said there was a good chance I would not last another six months and I would be dead if I continued with this behavior. So, I surrenderd my life to God again. My doctor gave me a chance and put me in a relapse prevention for 12 weeks, after which I have been clean and sober for 2 years and 6 months.

To this day I am clean and sober, and I plan to stay this way for ever but it wasn't easy. I had to learn James 4:6, 7, But he bestows a greater grace;

therefore, it says: "God resists the proud, but gives grace to the humble." So submit yourselves to God. Resist the devil, and he will flee from you.

We also need to learn Ephesians 6:10, 20, Finally, draw your strength from the Lord and from his mighty power. Put on the armor of God so that you may be able to stand firm against the tactics of the devil. For our struggle is not with flesh and blood but with the principalities, with the powers, with the world rulers of this present darkness, with the evil spirits in the heavens. Therefore, put on the armor of God, that you may be able to resist on the evil day and, having done everything, hold your ground So stand fast with your loins girded in truth, clothed with righteousness as a breastplate, and your feet shod in readiness for the gospel of peace. In all circumstances, hold faith as a shield, to quench all the flaming arrows of the evil one. And take the helmet of salvation and the sword of the Spirit, which is the word of God. With all prayer and supplication, pray at every opportunity in the Spirit. To that end, be watchful with all perseverance and supplication for all the holy ones and also for me, that speech may be given me to open my mouth, to make known with boldness the mystery of the gospel for which I am an ambassador in chains, so that I may have the courage to speak as I must.

CHAPTER 2

In James 4:8, "Draw near to God, and he will draw near to you. Cleanse your hands, you sinners, and purify your hearts, you of two minds.

In James 1:6, 8, But he should ask in faith, not doubting, for the one that doubts is like the wave of the sea that is driven and tossed about by the wind. For that person must not suppose that he will receive anything from the Lord, since he is a man of two minds, unstable in all his ways.

In James 1:12, 17, Blessed is the man who perseveres in temptation, for when he has been proved he will receive the crown of life that he promised to those who love him. No one experiencing temptation should say, "I am being tempted by God; for God is not subject to temptation to evil, and he himself tempts no one. Rather, each person is tempted when he is lured and enticed by his own desire. Then desire conceives and brings forth sin, and when sin reaches maturity it gives birth to death. Do not be deceived, my beloved brothers: all good giving and every perfect gift is from above, coming down from the Father of lights, with whom there is no alteration or shadow caused by change.

So what happens when people sin and what are the consequences of sin?

In Genesis 3:1, 6, Now the snake was the most cunning of all the wild animals that the Lord God had made. He asked the woman, "Did God really say, 'You shall not eat from any of the trees in the garden?' The woman answered the snake, "We may eat of the fruit of the trees in the garden; it is only about the fruit of the tree in the middle of the garden that

God said, 'You shall not eat it or even touch it, or else you will die." But the snake said to the woman: You certainly will not die! God knows well that when you eat of it your eyes will be opened and you will be like gods, who know good and evil. The woman saw that the tree was good for food and pleasing to the eyes, and the tree was desirable for gaining wisdom. So she took some of its fruit and ate it; and she also gave some to her husband, who was with her, and he ate it.

Now if we were to separate Adam and Eve's sin from its context, few of us would convict them of great transgression. All they did was swallow some fruit from a tree with a "do not eat" sign. Today, people think nothing of ignoring commands even biblical ones.

But God has a totally different view of our sins, each one is followed by negative consequences. Adam and Eve's disobedience led to pain and frustration in two basic areas of fulfillment - relationships and meaningful work. The whole earth fell under sin's curse, and all people born since then have entered the world with a sin nature that separates them from the Lord.

So what I'm trying to explain to everyone is that there are consequences for the sins we commit.

Here is another story in the bible that involves Satan. Any time you listen to Satan or any type of evil, if you act on it, there is a good chance you could get into trouble with the law of the land, or it might be that you could be in hot water with God Almighty, Jesus Christ, and all the Angels in Heaven. This next story will explain what I'm talking about.

In 1st Chronicles Chapter 21: 1, A satan rose up against Israel, and he incited David to take a census of Israel.

In 2nd Samuel 24:2, 25, The King therefore said to Joab and the leaders of the army who were with him, "tour all the tribes of Israel from Dan to Beer-sheba and register the people, that I may know their number." But Joab replied to the king: May the Lord your God increase the number of people hundredfold for my lord the king to see if with his own eyes. By why does it please my lord to do a thing of this kind?" However, the king's command prevailed over Joab and the leaders of the army, so they left the king's presence in order to register the people of Israel. Crossing the Jordan, they began near Aroer, south of the city in the wadi, and turned in the direction of Gad toward Jazer. They continued on to Gilead and to the district below Mount Hermon. They they proceeded Dan; from there they turned toward Sidon, going to the fortress of Tyre and to all the cities of the Hivites and Canaanites, and ending up on the Negeb of Judah, at Beer-sheba. Thus, they toured the whole land, reaching Jerusalem again after nine months and twenty days. Joab then reported the census figures to the king: of men capable of wielding a sword, there were in Israel eight hundred thousand, and in Judah five hundred thousand.

Afterward, however, David regretted having numbered the people. David said to the Lord: "I have sinned grievously in what I have done. Take away, Lord, your servant's guilt, for I have acted very foolishly." When David rose in the morning, the word of the Lord came to the prophet Gad, David's seer, saying: Go, tell David: Thus says the Lord: I am offering you three options; choose one of them, and I will give you that. He asked: "Should three years of famine come upon your land; or three months of fleeing from your enemy while he pursues you; or is it to be three days of plague in your land? Now consider well: what answer am I to give to him who sent me?" David answered Gad: "I am greatly distressed. But let us fall into the hand of God, whose mercy is great, rather than into human hands. Thus David chose the plague. At the time of the wheat harvest it broke out among the people. The Lord sent a plague over Israel from morning until the time appointed, and from Dan to Beer-sheba seventy thousand of the people died. But when the angel stretched forth his hand toward Jerusalem to destroy it, the Lord changed his mind about the calamity, and said to the angel causing the destruction among the people: Enough now! Stay your hand. The angel of the Lord was then standing at the threshing floor of Araunah the Jebusite. When David saw the angel who was striking the people, he said to the Lord: "It was I who have sinned; it is I, the shepherd who have done wrong. But these sheep, what have they done wrong? Strike me and my father's family!"

On the same day Gad went to David and said to him, "Go ahead and set up an altar to the Lord on the threshing floor of Araunah the Jebusite. According to Gad's word, David went up as the Lord commanded. Now Araunah looked down and saw the king and his servants coming toward him while he was threshing wheat. So he went out and bowed down before the king, his face to the ground. Then Araunah asked, "Why does my lord the king come to his servant?" David replied, "To buy the threshing floor from you, to build an altar to the Lord, that the plague may be withdrawn from the people." But Araunah said to David, "Let my lord the king take it and offer up what is good in his sight. See, here are the oxen

See here are the oxen for burnt offerings, and the threshing sledges and the yokes of oxen for wood. All this does Araunah give to the king." Araunah then said to the king, "May the Lord your God accept your offering." The king, however, replied to Araunah, "No, I will buy it from you at the proper price, for I cannot sacrifice to the Lord my God burnt offerings that cost me nothing." So, David bought the threshing floor and the oxen for fifty silver shekels. Then David built an altar to the Lord there and sacrificed burnt offerings and communion offerings. The Lord granted relief to the land, and the plague was withdrawn from Israel.

The Temptation of Jesus in the wilderness. You can read in the books of Matthew 4:1, 4, Mark 1:12, 13, and in Luke 4:1, 4.

In the Book of Matthew 4:1, 11, Then Jesus was led by the Spirit into the desert to be tempted by the devil. He fasted for forty days and forty nights, and afterwards he was hungry. The tempter approached and said to him, "If you are the Son of God, command that these stones becomes loaves of bread." He said in reply, "It is written: 'One does not live by bread alone, but by every word that comes forth from the mouth of God.' Then, the devil took him to the holy city, and made him stand on the parapet of the temple, and said to him, "If you are the Son of God, throw yourself down." For it is written: 'He will command his angels concerning you' and 'with their hands they will support you, lest you dash your foot against a stone'. Jesus answered him, "Again it is written, 'You shall not put the Lord, your God, to the test.' Then the devil took him up to a very high mountain, and showed him all the kingdoms of the world in their magnificence, and he said to him, "All these I shall give to you, if you will prostrate yourself and worship me." At this, Jesus said to him, "Get away, Satan! It is written: 'The Lord your God, shall you worship and him alone shall you serve.' Then the devil left him and, behold, angels came and ministered to him.

John the Baptist in Matthew 3:1, 12, In those days John the Baptist appeared, preaching in the desert of Judea and saying, "Repent, for the kingdom of heaven is at hand!" It was of him that the prophet Isaiah had spoken when he said: "A voice of one crying out in the desert, 'Prepare the way of the Lord, make straight his paths.' John wore clothing made of camel's hair and had a leather belt around his waist. His food was locusts and wild honey. At that time Jerusalem, all Judea, and the whole region around the Jordan were going out to him and were being baptized by him in the Jordan River as they acknowledged their sins.'

When he saw many of the Pharisees and Sadducees coming to his baptism, he said to them, "You brood of vipers! Who warned you to flee from the coming wrath? Produce good fruit as evidence of your repentance. And do not presume to say to yourselves, 'We have Abraham as our Father.' For I tell you, God can raise up children to Abraham from these stones. Even now the ax lies at the root of the trees. Therefore, every tree that does not bear good fruit will be cut down and thrown into the fire. I am baptizing you with water, for repentance, but the one who is coming after me is mightier than I. I am not worthy to carry his sandals. He will baptize you with the holy Spirit and fire.'

Genesis 3:

Adam and Eve in the Garden of Eden. Read about the creation of Adam and Eve and how Satan, disguised as a serpent, tempted Eve to sin and eat the fruit from the tree of good and evil.

Ezekiel 28, and Isaiah 14.

Let's briefly look at both of these books. The story of Lucifer's Fall is described in two key Old Testament chapters. It would seem from the context of Ezekiel 28 that the first ten verses of this chapter are dealing with a human leader. Then, starting in verse 11 and on through verse 19, Lucifer is the focus of discussion.

The fall of Lucifer in the Bible

What is the rationale for the conclusion that these latter verses refer to the fall of Lucifer? Whereas the first ten verses in this chapter speak about the ruler of Tyre (who was condemned for claiming to be a god though he was just a man), the discussion moves to the King of Tyre starting in verse 11. Many scholars believe that though there was a human "ruler" of Tyre, the real "King" of Tyre was Satan, for it was he who was ultimately at work in this anti-God city and it was he who worked through the human ruler of the city.

Some have suggested that these verses may actually be dealing with a human King of Tyre who was empowered by Satan. Perhaps the King of Tyre was a tool of Satan, possibly even indwelt by Satan. Perhaps the historic King of Tyre was a tool of Satan, possibly even indwelt by him. In describing this King, Ezekiel also gives us glimpses of the superhuman creature, Satan, who was using, if not indwelling him.

Now there are things that are true of this "King" that - at least ultimately - cannot be said to be true of human being. For example, the King is portrayed as having a different nature from man (he is a cherub, verse 14); he had a different position from man (he was blameless and sinless, verses 15); he was in a different realm from man (the holy mount of God, verses 13, 14); he received a different judgment from man (he was cast out of the mountain of God and thrown to the earth, verse 16); and the superlatives used to describe him don't seem to fit that of a normal human being ("full of wisdom," "perfect in beauty," and having "the seal of perfection," verse 12 NASB).

Who is Lucifer, why did He Rebel?

Our text tells us that this King was a created being and left the creative hand of God in a perfect state (Ezekiel 28:12, 15). And he remained perfect in his ways until iniquity was found in him (verse 15). What was this iniquity? We read in verse 17, your heart became proud on account of your beauty, and you corrupted your wisdom because of your splendor." Lucifer apparently became so impressed with his own beauty, intelligence, power, and position that he began to desire for himself the honor and glory that belonged to God alone. The sin that corrupted Lucifer was self-generated pride.

Apparently, this represents the actual beginning of sin in the universe - preceding the fall of the human Adam by an indeterminate time - Sin originated in the free will of Lucifer in which - with full understanding of the issues involved he chose to rebel against the creator.

This mighty angelic being was rightfully judged by God: "I threw you to the earth" (Ezekiel 28:18). This doesn't mean that Satan had no further access to heaven, for other scripture verses clearly indicate that Satan maintained this access even after his fall (Job 1:6-12; Zechariah 3:1, 2). However, Ezekiel 28:18 indicates that Satan was absolutely and completely cast out of God's heavenly government and his place of authority (Luke 10:18)

Isaiah 14:12, 17 is another Old Testament passage that may refer to the fall of Lucifer. We must be frank in admitting that some Bible scholars see no reference whatsoever to Lucifer in this passage. It is argued that the being mentioned in this verse is referred to as a man (Isaiah 14:16); is compared with other Kings on the earth (verse 18); and the words, "How you have fallen from heaven" (verse 12) is alleged to refer to a fall from great political heights.

There are other scholars who interpret this passage as referring only to the fall of Lucifer, with no reference whatsoever to a human king. The argument here is that the description of this being is beyond humanness and hence could not refer to a mere mortal man.

There is a third view that I think is preferable to the views above. This view sees Isaiah 14:12-17 as having a dual reference. It may be that verses 4 through 11 deal with an actual King of Babylon. Then, in verses 12 through 17, we find a dual reference that includes not just the King of Babylon but a typological description of Lucifer as well.

If this passage contains a reference to the fall of Lucifer, then the pattern of this passage would seem to fit that of the Ezekiel 28 reference - that is, first a human leader is described, and then dual reference is made to a human leader and Satan.

It is significant that the language used to describe this being fits other passages in the Bible that speak about Satan. For example, the five "I will's" in Isaiah 14 indicate an element of pride, which was also evidenced in Ezekiel 28:17. Timothy 3:6 which makes reference to Satan's conceit.

As a result of this heinous sin against God, Lucifer was banished from living in heaven Isaiah 14:12. He became corrupt, and his name changed from Lucifer (morning star) to Satan ("adversary"). His power became completely perverted Isaiah 14:12, 17. And his destiny, following the second coming of Jesus Christ, is to be bound in a pit during the 1000-year millennial kingdom over which Jesus Christ will rule Revelation 20:3, and eventually will be thrown into the lake of fire Matthew 25:41.

A lesson from the Last Moments of Jesus Christ life in the Book of Luke chapter 22 and 23.

Overall point: The major battle we face in this life is not what is seen, but what is not seen - Satan is intensely and intentionally opposed to what God is doing. And the greatest defense we have is not our offense, but rather our dependence. Jesus is prayerful and successful; the disciples are prayerless and care less.

First, we must understand from this story in Luke chapter 22, and 23 that Satan intensely and intentionally opposes what God is doing in this world. In the last moments of Jesus' life, it is remarkable how many times Satan is found in the story in obvious ways, much less how much he is found lurking behind the scenes. In Luke 22:3 we read that Satan enters Judas. We could discuss the views on what this means, but it is not important for our purposes. For now, simply note that Satan is actively working against God's purposes, seeking to destroy the Messiah. In Luke 22:31, we find that Jesus makes it clear that Satan wants to sift like wheat the disciples. Although Jesus is talking directly to Simon Peter, the "you" in verse 31 of Luke, is in the plural form, which identifies all of the disciples as the target, in verse 32 it is singular, so the comment is directed toward Peter. The verb has the idea of pick you to pieces! or "tear you apart" or ruin you! Satan aggressively wants to destroy these followers of Jesus, seemingly putting to death any momentum Jesus might have gained in drawing people to himself. Finally, in Luke 22:53, we see that the power of darkness seems to be winning the day, which will culminate in the death of Jesus on the cross. This calls our attention back to Luke 4, The temptation of Jesus. Satan even actively sought to lure Jesus away from the path that had been laid out for him by the Father.

This intense and intentional opposition of Satan to God's purposes extends to us as well. In 1 Peter 5:8, Peter warns the believers who are under persecution to be on the alert because our "opponent the devil prowls around like a roaring lion, seeking someone to devour." In other words, he wants to tear us to pieces as well. Like a lion in its natural habitat, he sits back and looks for the vulnerable and weak so that he might devour his prey. Ephesian 6:10, 12 underscores this struggle as well. "Our struggle is not with 'flesh and blood' but with the principalities, with the powers, with the world rulers of this present darkness, with the evil spirits in the heavens." Ephesians 6:13 adds "therefore, put on the armor of God, that you may be able to resist on the evil day and, having done everything, to hold your ground." Ephesians 6:16 encourages us "in all circumstances, hold faith as a shield, to quench all the flaming arrows of the evil one." We are in a battle, daily, until Jesus returns.

Second, we can note the strategies that are used in this story to prepare for the battle. I want us to see the contrast between Jesus' preparation and the disciples' preparation. I want to begin with the disciples. In Luke chapters 22, and 23, after Jesus warns the disciples (the "you" is plural) and Peter (Jesus is addressing Peter) that Satan is after them, Peter basically states, "Bring it on!" He cannot imagine a scenario in which he might deny Jesus. He announces his willingness to even go to prison or to die, but he will never deny Jesus. We find a similar conviction in all of the disciples in Luke 22:22, 24. After Jesus announces that one of them is going to betray him, they are speechless. They cannot imagine being at a place where they would consider betraying Jesus, much less actually doing it. In fact, their discussion turns into a debate about which of them is the greatest. Their questioning turns to arrogance.

They believe that they are strong, even the strongest in the bunch, but they are weak. Knowing their vulnerability, in Luke 22:40, Jesus calls them to pray so that they will not be lured away from their conviction of faithfulness. However, they slept. Peter and all of the disciples are in a vulnerable place and eventually lose their battle, succumbing to temptation. They all scatter from Jesus! The disciples are prayerless and careless.

Jesus is the contrast of the disciples. The intensity of what he is about to encounter will be far more intense than anything the disciples could ever imagine. However, in Luke chapter 22:41, 44, we find Jesus pouring out his heart in prayer as he wants to please his Father and continue in faithfulness. He recognizes his dependency, and in the end, he successfully fulfills his mission and goes to the cross to die for our sins in obedience to his Father. Jesus is prayerful and successful.

Prayer is strategic for any follower of Jesus. In Luke 22:40, 46, Jesus had warned the disciples of their best plan of attack. They are to pray. In the end, we find that they are ready for physical violence but not the spiritual battle. See Luke 22:38, 49-50. The application for us is found in Ephesians 6:10, 18. Paul encourages the church with these words, praying at all times in the spirit, which is the word of God, will all prayer and supplication... making supplication for the saints." His point is that we must be battle ready! We continue the Lord's work until Jesus returns. Prayer must be an important part of our lives. Today, Jesus' words echo to us, "Pray that you do not enter into temptation."

I find that prayer suffers in the lives of many, if not most, Christians. As a result, our lives probably look more like the disciples who were found sleeping, and eventually fell away! Let's learn a lesson from their lives. Let's honestly answer the questions: Does prayer exist in your life? Are we engaging this battle that we cannot see by coming before the throne in prayer? And I mean prayer that does battle against the lusts of the flesh that wage war against the soul, that does battle against the pleasures, riches, and worries of this present age that can dominate our resources, that does battle against the course of this would that wants to suck us in, etc. Let's not follow the example of the disciples in Luke chapter 22 and 23, and be prayerless and, therefore, careless. Let's follow the example of Jesus and be prayerful and, therefore, successful... until Jesus comes!

Jesus is in heaven, and everything you have read about in chapter 21 of Revelation belongs to God Almighty and his Son Jesus Christ, and the bride (the Lamb's wife). The city of gold and the streets of gold, the New Jerusalem, the holy city. Revelations 21: 22, 27. I saw no temple in the city, for its temple is the Lord God almighty and the Lamb. The city had no need of sun or moon to shine on it, for the glory of God gave it light, and its lamp was the Lamb. The nations will walk by its light, and to it the kings of the earth will bring their treasure. During the day its gates will never be shut, and there will be no night there. The treasure and wealth of the nations will be brought there, but nothing unclean will enter it, nor any (one) who does abominable things or tells lies. Only those will enter whose names are written in the Lamb's book of life.

Ephesians 6:18, With all prayer and supplication, pray at every opportunity in the Spirit. To that end, be watchful with all perseverance and supplication for all the holy ones.

After describing the pieces of the armor of God, Paul adds another important part of spiritual battle, prayer. This is not a piece of spiritual armor yet is essential to winning spiritual battles. Why? Prayer connects us to the power of God, which is necessary to defeat spiritual enemies. Communication in battle is often the difference between victory and defeat. This is especially true when referring to soldiers hearing the instructions of their commander. Paul then notes some specific applications of Prayer in this verse and the next. First, believers are to pray in the spirit. Our prayers are not merely our thoughts or about our desires but are to be done in submission to God.

Next, we are to keep alert. While we may not be literally praying every waking second, there is never a good time to set prayer aside. It's a tool we need to have in constant use, 1ˢᵗ Thessalonians 5:1, Pray without ceasing.

Third, prayer is something to do "with all perseverance." We do not pray once each day and then stop. We are to talk with God continually and about all matters. Nothing is too big or too small to discuss with the Lord.

Finally, Paul highlights the importance of praying for the needs of other believers. We praise God in prayer, pray for our own needs, and also pray for the needs of others. Each of these areas is important.

Now I John Michael Gurule, pray every day, Hear our prayer. Oh, Lord, God, Almighty. Come bless our land. As we seek you.

CHAPTER 3

The Story of St. Michael The Archangel

Saint Michael the Archangel is referenced in the Old Testament and has been part of Christian teaching since the earliest times. In Catholic writing and traditions, he acts as the defender of the church, a chief opponent of Satan, and assists souls at the hour of death.

Saint Michael the Archangel Prayer: Defend us in battle. Be our protection against the wickedness and snares of the devil. May God rebuke him, we humbly pray, O Prince of the heavenly hosts, by the power of God, thrust into hell Satan and all evil spirits who wander through the world for the ruin of souls, Amen.

The Archangel Michael is mentioned five times in the New King James Version, according to the book of Daniel in 500 B.C. Daniel has a vision of a war against the Jewish people in Jerusalem, in (167-164 B.C.) you can read this story in the book of 1st Maccabees chapter 1 of the American Bible Society. It goes from Alexander the Great to Antiochus IV Epiphanes.

Saint Michael appears in Holy Scriptures as the Guardian of the Children of Israel, their comfort and protector in times of sorrow or conflict. I will go down the list in the St. Michael card and you will see that these scriptures are true.

The five scriptures that you can read about St. Michael the Archangel, you can study these scriptures starting with Revelation 12:7, Daniel 10:13, Daniel 10:21, Daniel 12:1, and Jude 1:9 these are scriptures that will turn into stories of how St. Michael the Archangel is the Guardian of the Children of Israel, their comfort and protector in times of sorrow or conflict.

So starting off with the first story on the card it reads:

St. Michael The Archangel

Michael, or who is like unto God? Such was the cry of the Great Archangel when he drove out the rebel Lucifer in the conflict of the heavenly hosts, and from that hour he has been known as "Michael," the captain of the armies of God, the type of divine fortitude, the champion of every faithful soul in strife with the power of evil. You can find the story in Revelation chapter 12:7, 9.

And war broke out in heaven: St. Michael and his angels fought with the dragon, and the dragon and his angels fought back, but they did not prevail, nor was a place found for them in heaven any longer. So the great dragon was cast to the earth, and his angels were cast out, that serpent of old, called the devil and Satan, who deceives the whole world: he was cast to the earth, and his angels were cast out with him.

St. Michael the Archangel is the guardian and protector of Israel. So the dragon was angry with the women, and went to make war with the saints, the women clothed with the sun, moon, and twelve stars symbolizes the people of Israel, is the Virgin Mary, who represents more than herself... for indeed Israel, like a Mother, brought forth the Messiah for all the nations. In the book of Genesis 32:27, 29, it speaks of the changes of names. The man then said, "Let me go, for it is daybreak." But Jacob said, "I will not let you go until you bless me." What is your name? the man asked. He answered, "Jacob." Then the man said, "You shall no longer be named Jacob, but Israel, because you have contended with divine and human beings and have prevailed." Jacob had twelve sons.

Now the second story in the St. Michael the Archangel card.

Thus, he appears in Holy Scripture as the guardian of the children of Israel, their comfort and protector in times of sorrow or conflict.

So, what I'm going to do is write about four different conflicts. Two conflicts between the Philistines and Israel, and two conflicts between the Arabs and Palestinians, against the Israelites.

The first conflict that I'm writing about is a story you can find in Judges 13, 14, 15, 16. The story of Samson and Delilah.

Samson was betrayed by his lover Delilah, who ordered a servant to cut his hair while he was sleeping and turned him over to his Philistine enemies, who gouged out his eyes and forced him to grind grain in a mill at Gaza. While there, his hair began to regrow.

Gaza is also mentioned in the Hebrew Bible as the place where Samson was imprisoned and met his death. The prophets Amos and Zephaniah are believed to have prophesied that Gaza would be deserted. According to biblical accounts, Gaza fell to Israelite rule, from the reign of King David in the early 11th century BCE. When the united Monarchy split in about 930 BCE, Gaza became a part of the northern kingdom of Israel. Gaza and the Palestinians.

During the 12th century BCE, the Philistines settled on the fertile coast of Palestine. They founded five city states (Ashdod, Ashkelon, Ekron, Gath and Gaza) which then formed a confederation; Palestine is named after their inhabitants as "Land of the Philistines."

What city did Samson destroy? Gaza. Samson lost his strength and he is captured by the Philistines who blind him by gouging out his eyes. They then take him to Gaza, imprison him, and put him to work turning a large millstone and grinding grain.

Samson is a Biblical figure who appears in the Book of Judges chapters 13 to 16. He was an Israelite who followed the proscriptions of Nazirite life, which included not drinking nor trimming his locks or hair. A man of tremendous strength, his power was taken from him after his lover Delilah cut his hair.

The Philistines were a group of people who arrived in the Levant (an area that includes modern-day Israel, Gaza, Lebanon and Syria) during the 12ᵗʰ century B.C.

So here is that story of Samson and Delilah in four chapters.

Judges 13: 1, 24, The Israelites again did what was evil in the sight of the Lord, who therefore delivered them into the power of the Philistines for forty years.

There was a certain man from Zorah, of the clan of the Danites, whose name was Manoah. His wife was barren and had borne no children. An angel of the Lord appeared to the woman and said to her: Though you are barren and have no children, you will conceive and bear a son. Now, then, be careful to drink no wine or beer and to eat nothing unclean, for you will conceive and bear a son. No razor shall touch his head, for the boy is to be a nazirite for God from the womb. It is he who will begin to save Israel from the power of the Philistines.

The woman went and told her husband, "A man of God came to me, he had the appearance of an angel of God, fearsome indeed. I did not ask him where he came from, nor did he tell me his name. But he said to me, 'You will conceive and bear a son. So drink no wine or beer, and eat nothing unclean. For the boy shall be a nazirite for God from the womb, until the day of his death.' Manoah then prayed to the Lord. "Please my Lord", he said, "may the man of God whom you sent return to us to teach us what to do for the boy who is to be born."

God heard the prayer of Manoah, and the angel of God came to the woman as she was sitting in the field; but her husband Manoah was not with her. The woman ran quickly and told her husband. "The man who came to me the other day has appeared to me," she said to him; so Manoah got up and followed his wife. When he reached the man, he said to him, "Are you the one who spoke to my wife?" I am, he answered. Then Manoah asked, "Now, when what you say comes true, what rules must the boy follow? What must he do? The angel of the Lord answered Manoah: Your wife must be careful about all the things of which I spoke to her. She must not eat anything unclean. Let her observe all that I have commanded her. Then Manoah said to the angel of the Lord, "Permit us to detain you, so that we may prepare a young goat for you." But the angel of the Lord answered Manoah: Though you detained me, I would not eat your food. But if you want to prepare a burnt offering, then offer it up to the Lord. For Manoah did not know that he was the angel of the Lord. Then Manoah said to the angel of the Lord, "What is your name, that we may honor you when your words come true?" The angel of the Lord answered him: Why do you ask my name? It is wondrous. Then Manoah took a young goat with a grain offering and offered it on the rock to the Lord, who works wonders. While Manoah and his wife were looking on, as the flame rose to the heavens from the altar, the angel of the Lord ascended in the flame of the altar. When Manoah and his wife saw this, they fell on their faces to the ground; but the angel of the Lord was seen no more by Manoah and his wife. Then Manoah, realizing that it was the angel of the Lord, said to his wife, "We will certainly die, for we have seen God." But his wife said to him, "If the Lord had mean to kill us, he would not have accepted a burnt offering and grain offering from our hands! Nor would he have let us see all this or hear what we have heard."

The woman bore a son and named him Samson, and when the boy grew up the Lord blessed him. The spirit of the Lord came upon him for the first time in Mahaneth-dan, between Zorah and Eshtaol.

Judges, 14: 1, 19, Samson went down to Timnah where he saw one of the Philistine women. On his return he told his father and mother, "I saw in Timnah a woman, a Philistine. Get her for me as a wife." His father and mother said to him, "Is there no woman among your kinsfolk or among all your people, that you must go and take a women from the uncircumcised Philistines?" But Samson answered his father, "Get her for me, for she is the one I want." Now his father and mother did not know that this had been brought about by the Lord, who was seeking an opportunity against the Philistines; for at that time they ruled over Israel.

So Samson went down to Timnah with his father and mother. When he turned aside to the vineyards of Timnah, a young lion came roaring out toward him. But the spirit of the Lord rushed upon Samson, and he tore the lion apart barehanded, as one tears a young goat. Without telling his father or mother what he had done, he went down and spoke to the woman. He liked her. Later, when he came back to marry her, he turned aside to look at the remains of the lion, and there was a swarm of bees in the lion's carcass, and honey. So he scooped the honey out into his hands and ate it as he went along. When he came to his father and mother, he gave them some to eat, but did not tell them that he had scooped the honey from the lion's carcass.

His father also went down to the woman, and Samson gave a feast there, since it was customary for the young men to do this. Out of their fear of him, they brought thirty men to be his companions. Samson said to them, "Let me propose a riddle to you. If within the seven days of the feast you solve it for me, I will give you thirty linen tunics and thirty set of garments. But if you cannot answer it for me, you must give me thirty linen tunics and thirty sets of garments. "Propose your riddle, they responded, and we will listen to it." So he said to them,

"Out of the eater came food,
out of the strong came sweetness."

For three days they were unable to answer the riddle, and on the fourth day they said to Samson's wife, "Trick your husband into solving the riddle for us, or we will burn you and your family. Did you invite us here to reduce us to poverty?" So Samson's wife wept at his side and said, "You must hate me! You do not love me! You proposed a riddle to my people but did not tell me the answer." He said to her, "If I did not tell even my father or my mother, must I tell you?" But she wept beside him during the seven days the feast lasted, and on the seventh day, he told her the answer, because she pressed him, and she explained the riddle to her people.

On the seventh day, before the sun set, the men of the city said to him,

"What is sweeter than honey,
what is stronger than a lion?"

He replied to them,

"If you had not plowed with my heifer,
you would not have solved my riddle."

The spirit of the Lord rushed upon him, and he went down to Ashkelon, where he killed thirty of their men and stripped them; he gave their garments to those who had answered the riddle. Then he went off to his own family in anger, and Samson's wife was married to the companion who had been his best man.

Judges 15: 1, 20, After some time, in the season of the wheat harvest, Samson visited his wife, bringing a young goat. But when he said, "Let me go into my wife's room," her father would not let him go in. He said, "I thought you hated her, so I gave her to your best man. Her younger sister is better; you may have her instead." Samson said to him, "This time I am guiltless if I harm the Philistines." So Samson went and caught three hundred jackals, and turning them tail to tail, he took some torches and tied one between each pair of tails. He then kindled the torches and set the jackals loose in the standing grain of the Philistines, thus burning both the shocks and standing grain, the vineyards and olive groves.

When the Philistines asked, "Who has done this?" they were told, "Samson, the son-in-law of the Timnite, because his wife was taken and given to his best man. So the Philistines went up and destroyed her and her family by fire. Samson said to them, "If this is how you act, I will not stop until I have taken revenge on you." And he struck them hip and thigh—a great slaughter. Then he went down and stayed in a cleft of the crag of Etam.

The Philistines went up and encamped in Judah, deploying themselves against Lehi. When the men of Judah asked, "Why have you come up against us?" they answered, "To take Samson prisoner; to do to him as he has done to us." Three thousand men of Judah went down to the cleft of the crag of Etam and said to Samson, "Do you not know that the Philistines are our rulers? Why, then, have you done this to us?" He answered them, "As they have done to me, so have I done to them." They said to him, "WE have come down to bind you and deliver you to the Philistines." Samson said to them, "Swear to me that you will not attack me yourselves." No, they replied, "we will only bind you and hand you over to them. We will certainly not kill you." So they bound him up from the crag. When he reached Lehi, and the Philistines came shouting to meet him: the ropes around his arms became like flax that is consumed by fire, and his bonds melted away from his hands. Coming from the fresh jawbone of an ass, he reached out, grasped it, and with it killed a thousand men. Then Samson said,

"With the jawbone of an ass
I have piled them in a heap;
With the jawbone of an ass
I have slain a thousand men.

As he finished speaking, he threw the jawbone from him, and so that place was named Ramath-lehi. Being very thirsty, he cried to the Lord and said, "You have put this great victory into the hand of your servant. Must I now die of thirst and fall into the hands of the uncircumcised?" Then God split the cavity in Lehi, and water issued from it, and Samson drank till his spirit returned and he revived. Hence it is called En-hakkore in Lehi to this day.

Samson judged Israel for twenty years in the days of the Philistines.

Chapter 16, 1, 31, Once Samson went to Gaza, where he saw a prostitute and visited her. The people of Gaza were told, "Samson has come here," and they surrounded him with an ambush at the city gate all night long. And all the night they waited, saying, "At morning light we will kill him." Samson lay there until midnight. Then he rose at midnight, seized the doors of the city gate and the two gateposts, and tore them loose, bar and all. He hoisted them on his shoulders and carried them to the top of the ridge opposite Hebron.

After that he fell in love with a woman in the Wadi Sorek who name was Delilah. The lords of the Philistines came up to her and said, "Trick him and find out where he gets his great strength, and how we may overcome and bind him so as to make him helpless. Then for our part, we will each give you eleven hundred pieces of silver.

So Delilah said to Samson, "Tell me where you get your great strength and how you may be bound so as to be made helpless." "If they bind me with seven fresh bowstrings that have not dried", Samson answered her, "I shall grow weaker and be like anyone else." So the lords of the Philistines brought her seven fresh bowstrings that had not dried, and she bound him with them. She had men lying in wait in the room, and she said to him, "The Philistines are upon you, Samson!" But he snapped the bowstrings as a thread of tow is snapped by a whiff of flame; and his strength remained unexplained.

Delilah said to Samson, "You have mocked me and told me lies. Now tell me how you may be bound." If they bind me tight with new ropes, with which no work has been done, he answered her, "I shall grow weaker and be like anyone else," So Delilah took new ropes and bound him with them. Then she said to him, "The Philistines are upon you, Samson!" For there were men lying in wait in the room. But he snapped the ropes of his arms like thread.

Delilah said to Samson again, "Up to now you have mocked me and told me lies. Tell me how you may be bound." He said to her, "If you weave the seven locks of my hair into the web and fasten them with the pin. I shall grow weaker and be like anyone else." So when he went to bed, Delilah took the seven locks of hair and wove them into the web, and fastened them with the pin. Then she said, "The Philistines are upon you, Samson!" Awakening from his sleep, he pulled out both the loom and the web.

Then she said to him, "How can you say 'I love you' when your heart is not mine? Three times already you have mocked me, and not told me where you get your great strength!" She pressed him continually and pestered him till he was deathly weary of it. So he told her all that was in his heart and said, "No razor has touched my head, for I have been a nazirite for God from my mother's womb. If I am shaved, my strength will leave3 me, and I shall grow weaker and be like anyone else." When Delilah realized that he had told her all that was in his heart, she summoned the lords of the Philistines, saying, "Come up this time, for he has told me all that is in his heart. So the lords of the Philistines came to her and brought the money with them. She put him to sleep on her lap and called for a man who shaved off the seven locks of his hair. He immediately became helpless, for his strength had left him. When she said, "The Philistines are upon you, Samson!" he woke from his sleep and thought, "I will go out as I have done time and again and shake myself free." He did not realize that the Lord had left him. But the Philistines seized him and gouged out his eyes. Then they brought him down to Gaza and bound him with bronze fetters, and he was put to grinding grain in the prison. But the hair of his head began to grow as soon as it was shaved.

The lord of the Philistines assembled to offer a great sacrifice to their god Dagon and to celebrate. They said, "Our god has delivered Samson our enemy into our power." When the people saw him, they praised their god. For they said,

"Our god has delivered into our power
our enemy, the ravager of our land,
the one who has multiplied our slain."

When their spirits were high, they said, "Call Samson that he may amuse us," So they called Samson from the prison, and he provided amusement for them. They made him stand between the columns, and Samson said to the attendant who was holding his hands, "Put me where I may touch the columns that support the temple, so that I may lean against them." The temple was full of men and women: all the lords of the Philistines were there, and from the roof about three thousand men and women looked on as Samson provided amusement. Samson cried out to the Lord and said, "Lord God, remember me! Strengthen me only this once that I may avenge myself on the Philistines at one blow for my two eyes," Samson grasped the two middle columns on which the temple rested and braced himself against them, one at his right, the other at his left. Then saying, "Let me die with the Philistines!" Samson pushed hard, and the temple fell upon the lords and all the people that were in it. Those he killed by his dying were more than those he had killed during his lifetime.

His kinsmen and all his father's house went down and bore him up for burial in the grave of Manoah his father between Zorah and Eshtoal. He had judged Israel for twenty years.

Another story about the Israelites and the Philistines, St Michael the Archangel and the Angels of God in the St Michael Card says he who appears in Holy Scripture as the guardian of the children of Israel, their comfort and protector in times of sorrow or conflict.

The David and Goliath Story in 1ˢᵗ Samuel Chapter 17.

Saul and the Israelites are facing the Philistines in the Valley of Elah. David hurls a stone from his sling and hits Goliath in the center of his forehead, Goliath falls on his face to the ground, and David cuts off his head.

Here is that story, 1ˢᵗ Samuel 17: 1, 58, The Philistines rallied their forces for battle of Socoh in Judah and camped between Socoh and Azekah at Ephes-dammim. Saul and the Israelites rallied and camped in the valley of the Elah, drawing up their battle line to meet the Philistines. The Philistines were stationed on one hill and the Israelites on an opposite hill, with a valley between them.

A champion named Goliath of Gath came out from the Philistine camp; he has six cubits and a span tall. He had a bronze helmet on his head and wore a bronze breastplate of scale armor weighing five thousand shekels, bronze greaves, and had a bronze scimitar slung from his shoulders. The shaft of his javelin was like a weaver's beam, and its iron head weighed six hundred shekels. He shield-bearer went ahead of him. He stood and shouted to the ranks of Israel: "Why come out in battle formation? I am a Philistine, and you are Saul's servants. Choose one of your men and have him come down to me. If he beats me in combat and kills me, we will be your vassals; but if I beat him and kill him, you shall be our vassals and serve us." The Philistine continued: "I defy the ranks of Israel today. Give me a man and let us fight together." When Saul and all Israel heard this challenge of the Philistine, they were stunned and terrified.

David was the son of an Ephrathite named Jesse from Bethlehem in Judah who had eight sons. In the days of Saul, Jesse was old and well on in years. The three oldest sons of Jesse had followed Saul to war; the names of these three sons who had gone off to war were Eliab the firstborn, Abinadab the second; and Shammah the third. David was the youngest. While the three oldest had joined Saul, David would come and go from Saul's presence to tend his father's sheep at Bethlehem.

Meanwhile the Philistine came forward and took his stand morning and evening for forty days.

Now Jesse said to his son David, "Take this ephah of roasted grain and these ten loaves for your brothers and bring them quickly to your brothers in the camp. Also take these ten cheeses for the field officer. Greet your brothers and bring home some token from them. Saul and your brothers, together with all Israel, are at war with the Philistines in the valley of the Elah." Early the next morning, having left the flock with a shepherd, David packed up and set out, as Jesse had commanded him. He reached the barricade of the camp just as the army, on their way to the battleground, were shouting their battle cry. The Israelites and the Philistines drew up opposite each other in battle array. David entrusted what he had brought to the keeper of the baggage and hastened to the battle line, where he greeted his brothers. While he was talking to them, the Philistine champion, by name Goliath of Gath, came up from the ranks of the Philistines and spoke as before, and David listened. When the Israelites saw the man, they all retreated before him, terrified. The Israelites had been saying, "Do you see this man coming up? He comes up to insult Israel. The king will make whoever kills him a very wealthy man. He will give his daughter to him and declare his father's family exempt from taxes in Israel. David now said to the men standing near him: "How will the man who kills this Philistine and frees Israel from disgrace be rewarded? Who is this uncircumcised Philistine that he should insult the armies of the living God?" They repeated the same words to him and said, "That is how the man who kills him will be rewarded." When Eliab, his oldest brother, heard him speaking with the men, he grew angry with David and said: "Why did you come down? With whom have you left those sheep in the wilderness? I know your arrogance and dishonest heart. You came down to enjoy the battle!" David protested, "What have I done now? I was only talking." He turned from him to another and asked the same question; and everyone gave him the same answer as before. The words that David had spoken were overheard and reported to Saul, who send for him.

Then David spoke to Saul: "My lord should not lose heart. Let your servant go and fight this Philistine." But Saul answered David, "You cannot go up against this Philistine and fight with him, for you are only a youth, while he has been a warrior from his youth." Then David told Saul: "Your servant used to tend his father's sheep, and whenever a lion or bear came to carry off a sheep from the flock, I would chase after it, attack it, and snatch the prey from its mouth. If it attacked me, I would seize it by the throat, strike it, and kill it. Your servant has killed both a lion and a bear. This uncircumcised Philistine will be as one of them, because he has insulted the armies of the living God."

David continued, "The same Lord who delivered me from the claws of the lion and the bear will deliver me from the hand of this Philistine." Saul answered David, "Go! The Lord will be with you."

Then Saul dressed David in his own tunic, putting a bronze helmet on his head and arming him with a coat of mail. David also fastened Saul's sword over his tunic. He walked with difficulty, however, since he had never worn armor before. He said to Saul, "I cannot go in these, because I am not used to them." So, he took them off. Then, staff in hand, David selected five smooth stones from the wadi and put them in the pocket of his shepherd's bag. With his sling in hand, he approached the Philistine.

With his shield-bearer marching before him, the Philistine advanced closer and closer to David. When he sized David up and saw that he was youthful, ruddy, and handsome in appearance, he began to deride him. He said to David, "Am I a dog that you come against me with a staff?" Then the Philistine cursed David by his gods and said to him, "Come here to me, and I will feed your flesh to the birds of the air and the beasts of the field." David answered him, "You come against me with sword and spear and scimitar, but I come against you in the name of the Lord of hosts, the God of the armies of Israel whom you have insulted. Today the Lord shall deliver you into my hand: I will strike you down and cut off your head. This very day I will feed your dead body and the dead bodies of the Philistine army to the birds of the air and the beasts of the field; thus the whole land shall learn that it is not by sword or spear that the Lord saves. For the battle belongs to the Lord, who shall deliver you into our hands.

The Philistine then moved to meet David at close quarters, while David ran quickly toward the battle line to meet the Philistine. David put his hand into the bag and took out a stone, hurled it with the sling, and struck the Philistine on the forehead. The stone embedded itself in his brow, and he fell on his face to the ground. Thus David triumphed over the Philistine with sling and stone; he struck the Philistine dead, and did it without a sword in his hand. Then David ran and stood over him; with the Philistine's own sword which he drew from its sheath he killed him and cut off his head.

When the Philistines saw that their hero was dead, they fled. Then the men of Israel and Judah sprang up with a battle cry and pursued them to the approaches of Gath and to the gates of Ekron, and Philistines fell wounded along the road from Shaaraim as far as Gath and Ekron. When they returned from the pursuit of the Philistines, the Israelites looted their camp. David took the head of the Philistine and brought it to Jerusalem; but he kept Goliath's armor in his own tent.

As Saul watched David go out to meet the Philistines, he asked his general Abner, "Abner, whose son is that young man?" Abner replied, "On your life, O King, I have no idea." And the king said, "Find out whose son the lad is." So when David returned from slaying the Philistine, Abner escorted him into Saul's presence. David was still holding the Philistine's head. Saul then asked him, "Whose son are you, young man?" David replied, "I am the son of your servant Jesse of Bethlehem."

CHAPTER 4

Still, second part of the story on the St Michael, Archangel Card. Thus he appears in Holy Scripture as guardian of the children of Israel, their comfort and protector in times of sorrow or conflict.

Now there is another war in 1948, Arab-Palestinian-Israel conflict. Is Palestine and Philistine the same? The area contained the five cities (the Pentapolis) of the Philistine confederacy (Gaza, Ashkelon (Ascalon), Ashdod, Gath, and Ekron) and was known as Philista, or the Land of the Philistines. It was from this designation that the whole of the country was later called Palestine by the Greeks. The word "Palestinian" derives from the Philistines, a people who were not indigenous to Canaan but who had gained control of the coastal plains of what are now Israel and Gaza for a time. According to ancient Egyptian records of the period, which is the first written mention of them, the Philistines reached the region in around the 12 century BCE, which the archeological record seem to confirm. The Palestinians don't see themselves as descendants of the Biblical invaders, but they are named for the Philistines just the same.

The Palestinian Exodus

This war in 1948, the Arab-Palestinian - Israel conflict, the introduction into this situation starts with Great Britain, during the early 20th century, promised the Jews a national home in Palestine, even though the overwhelming majority of the existing population consisted of non-Jews (Palestinians), the seeds for an ongoing conflict have been sown. With the support of the British Mandatory during the British Mandate of Palestine, the influx of Jewish settlers into Palestine increased. During the Unite Nations Mandate of Palestine, a partition plan on the basis of which the mandate of Palestine would be divided into a newly established Jewish State and an Arab State was presented The approval of this resolution by the UN General Assembly paved the way for the establishment of the State of Israel in 1948. Meanwhile a sophisticated campaign of ethnic cleaning of the Palestinian population was under way, which was meant to ensure that the demographic structure of the new state would favor Jews. These events, which Palestinians call the "Nakba" (catastrophe), led to a huge exodus of Palestinians from their homes and their displacement to other parts of Palestine and neighboring countries. The 1948 Arab-Israeli war was the second and final stage of the 1947-1949 Palestine war. It formally began following the end of the British Mandate for Palestine at midnight on 14 May 1948.

The starting was May 15, 1948, Location: British Mandate of Palestine, Sinai Peninsula, Southern Lebanon, The End of War was March 10, 1949. The war lasted 9 months, 3 weeks, and 2 days. So, in 1948, Israel was officially declared an independent state with David Ben Gurion, the head of the Jewish Agency, as the prime minister. While this historic event seemed to be a victory for Jews, it also marked the beginning of more violence with the Arabs. On the eve of May 14, the Arabs launched an air attack of the former Palestinian mandate by Arab armies from Lebanon, Syria, Iraq, and Egypt. Saudi Arabia sent a formation that fought under the Egyptian command. Five Arabs nations-immediately invaded the region in what became known as the 1948 Arab-Israel War. The war ended with Israeli forces controlling approximated 78 percent of historical Palestine. The remaining 22 percent fell under the administration of Egypt and Jordan. In 1967, Israel absorbed the whole of historical Palestine, as well as additional territory from Egypt and Syria. So why did Britain give Palestine to Israel? What is the Balfour Declaration? The Balfour Declaration ("Balfour's promise" in Arabic) was a public pledge by Britain in 1917 declaring its aim to establish a national home for the Jewish people in Palestine. How much land did Israel gain after the 1948 war? The UN partition promised 56 percent of British Palestine for the Jewish state; by the end of the war, Israel possessed 77 percent everything except the West

Bank and the eastern quarter of Jerusalem (controlled by Jordan), as well as the Gaza Strip (controlled by Egypt).

Events leading to the Six Day War (1967)

The road to war was paved by the growing tension in the area since 1963 over the issue of exploiting the water of the Joran River and the Kineret Lake. This led to an escalation of military clashes initiated by Syria, and to an increase of Palestinian terror attacks against Israel encouraged by Arab states, particularly Syria. The immediate causes for the war included a series of escalating steps taken by the Arabs; the concluding of a Syrian-Egyptian military pact to which Jordan and Iraq later joined, the expulsion of the UN Emergency Force (UNEF) from The Sinai Peninsula and the concentration of Egyptian forces there, and finally the closure by Egypt of the Straits of Tiran to Israeli shipping, constituting a casus belli for Israel. When Jordan, Iraq, Saudi Arabia, Syria and Lebanon moved their forces toward the Israeli border, Israel mobilized its reserve forces, and launched a diplomatic campaign to win international support to end the Egyptian blockade of Israeli shipping. When this failed and in reaction to Arab threats of wiping Israel out, the war began with an Israeli pre-emptive aerial strike of 5 June 1967. It ended on 10 June 1967 with Israel's victory. Meanwhile, a sophisticated campaign of ethnic cleansing, of the Palestinian population was under way, which was meant to ensure that the demographic structure of the new state would favor Jews. These events, which Palestinians call the "Nakba" (catastrophe), led to a huge exodus of Palestinians from their homes and their displacement to other parts of Palestine and neighboring countries. 1967 Palestinian exodus.

During the June war of 1967, Israel conquered the West Bank, East Jerusalem, Gaza, and the Golan Heights, territories where the settlement of Jews from all over the world was encouraged, at the expense of the remaining Palestinian population, Israeli Jewish settlements were erected with the support of the state of Israel, leading to an increase of the Israeli Jewish population in the Palestinian territories (West Bank, including East Jerusalem) from 600 Israeli settlers in 1968 to more than 550,000 in 2015, according to the Humanitarian Atlas of the United Nations Office for the Coordination of Humanitarian Affairs (UNOCHA) in Palestine. Where do these Palestinians refugees live? Nearly one-third of the registered Palestine refugees, more than 1.5 million individuals, live in 58 recognized Palestine refugee camps in Jordan, Lebanon, the Syrian Arab Republic, the Gaza Strip and the West Bank, including East Jerusalem. How many UNRWA Palestinian refugees are there? 5.6 million Palestine, as of 2019, over 5.6 million Palestine refugees were registered as such with the Agency and eligible to access its services within the UNRWA areas of operation. What is UNRWA, they provide assistance and protection for some 5.6 million registered Palestine refugees to help them achieve their full potential in human development. The United Nations Relief and Works Agency for Palestine Refugees (UNRWA) is funded almost entirely by voluntary contributions from UN Member States. UNRWA was created in 1949 to assist Palestine refugees.

Every day, 30,000 UNRWA teachers, doctors, nurses, social workers and many others serve their communities in Lebanon, Syria, Jordan, the West Bank and Gaza. Our work is only possible thanks to the support of donors, host countries, partners and individuals. Palestine refugees need more than just aid, they need a just solution. I and many others can pray for the Palestinians refugees, men, women, and children, we pray for a solution Amen. These children go to UNRWA schools. They provided good education. If these schools close, I can't afford to send them private schools. And public schools are already overcrowded (some 1 hear have 3 shifts). The consequences are catastrophic. If the money from the US stops what happens to the Palestinians refugees.

How much does the US give to Palestine?

In 2016, the United States contributed $368 million to the agency, and $350 million in 2017, but has cut around one third of its contributions for 2018. In January 2018, the United States withheld $65 million, roughly half the amount due in the month, again creating a financial crisis for UNRWA.

Why does the United States support Palestine?

The United States does not recognize the State of Palestine but accepts the Palestine Liberation Organization (PLO) as a representative of the

Palestinian people and the Palestinian National Authority as the authority legitimately governing the Palestinian territories under the Oslo Accords.

Answer and Explanation: Per the Oslo Accords, Israel was to withdraw from Jericho, Gaza, and the West Bank; Palestinians in such regions were granted some autonomy.

Who signed the Oslo Accords?

In 1994 Israeli Prime Minister Yitzhak Rabin, Israeli Foreign Minister Shimon Peres, and PLO Chairman Yasser Arafat received the Nobel Peace Prize following the signing on the Oslo Accords, for their efforts to create peace in the Middle East.

Did the Oslo Accords succeed or fail?

The Oslo process is the "peace process" that started in 1993 with secrets talks between Israel and the PLO ... peace process. A number of agreements were reached, until the Oslo process ended after the failure of the Camp David Summit in 2000 and the Outbreak of the Second Intifada.

What does the intifada symbolize?

The Arabic word intifada translates literally as shake, shaking, or shake off. In the context of Arab-Israeli violence it refers to a concerned Palestinian attempt to shake off Israeli power and gain independence.

Israel-Palestine conflict: The intifadas, explained. May 18, 2018, There has been a wave of mainly stabbing attacks by Palestinians. The intifadas were two Palestinian uprising against Israel.

The intifadas were two Palestinian uprising against Israel, the first in the late 1980's and the second in the early 2000's.

What was the third intifada?

The 2014 Jerusalem unrest, sometimes referred as the Silent Intifada (other names given include urban intifada, firecracker intifada, car intifada,

Jerusalem intifada, and Third intifada) is a term occasionally used to refer to an increase in violence focused on Jerusalem in 2014, especially from July of that year.

Intifada is a sustained series of Palestinian protests, and in some cases violent riots, against the Israeli occupation of the West Bank that had begun twenty years prior, in 1967.

Israeli settlements currently exit in the Palestinian territory of the West Bank, including East Jerusalem, and in the Syrian territory of the Golan Heights, and had previously existed within the Egyptian territory of the Sinai Peninsula, and within the Palestinian territory of the Gaza Strip; Israel did conquer these territories.

Why is Israel allowed to occupy Palestine?

Instead of exchanging land for peace, as per UN Resolution 242 that called on Israel to give up the territories in exchange for peace with its neighbors at the end of the 1967 War. Israel began encouraging its citizens to move into territories it occupied and supporting them as they did so.

Israel's security concerns - although security is a fundamental Israel preoccupation, the state has never formalized an official national security policy or doctrine. Before June 1967, the Israeli Cabinet did not regard the West Bank as having a vital security value.

Can Palestinians be citizens of Israel?

Arab citizens of Israel, or Arab Israelis, are Israeli citizens who are Arab. Many Arab citizens of Israel self-identify as Palestinian and commonly self-designate themselves as Palestinian citizens of Israeli Palestinians.

Despite many rounds of negotiation between Palestinians and Israelis under the auspices of several parties, including the United States, the two sides have failed to reach a resolution of the conflict. The so-called two state solution (a viable independent Palestinian state border the State of Israel), which is the option preferred by the international community, is in 2015. Further away than ever.

Meanwhile, Israel tolerated by the international community, continues to expand its settlements on the West Bank and in East Jerusalem while denying Palestinians their inalienable rights to national independence, sovereignty, and self -determination.

Widespread protests leading to violent clashes with the Israeli Security Forces were accompanied by almost daily stabbings or attempted stabbing of Israelis by young Palestinians in both the West Bank and Israel. According to UNOCHA, between 1 October and 30 November, 103 Palestinians including 23 children, were killed during shooting and other clashes with Israeli citizens and were stabbed to death.

Israeli-Palestinian conflict: What is Hamas? May 14, 2018 Hamas is a Palestinian Islamist political organization and militant group. A Sunni-Islamic militant group. The militant wing of Hamas has launched attacks against Israeli civilians and soldiers.

In 2006, Hamas won the 2006 Palestinian legislative elections and assumed administrative control of Gaza Strip and West Bank. To date, the Hamas government is only economically bonded with the Ramal-based Palestinian National Authority, performing the governing over the Gaza Strip independently.

Why is Gaza firing rockets into Israel?

Israeli Response to Gaza Rockets Signals Hamas to Rein in Islamic Jihad. The barrage of rockets fired Friday night from the Gaza Strip into Israel seem to have been launched by the Palestinian Islamic Jihad group. Nov 2, 2019.

On 12 November, the Palestinian Islamic Jihad (PIJ) fired 190 rockets into Israel from the Gaza Strip, including long-range rockets fired towards Tel Aviv, leading to several civilians being wounded. This was in response to the targeted killing by Israel of senior PIJ Commander Baha Abu al-Ata in Gaza.

Where does Hamas get its rockets?

Palestinian rockets include those locally made in Gaza and the West Bank as well as weapons smuggled from Iran and Syria. Rockets are used in attacks on Israel, mostly to target Israeli civilian centers in addition to Israel military posts.

How often are rockets fired into Israel?

More than 200 rockets fired into Israel from Gaza; Israel responds, killing 3. May 4, 2019.

Does Hamas recognize Israel?

The 2017 charter accepted for the first time the idea of a Palestinian State within the borders that existed before 1967 and rejects recognition of Israel which it terms as the "Zionist enemy." It advocates such a state as transitional but also advocated liberation of all of Palestine."

Why is Gaza dangerous?

Israeli officials say the blockade is necessary to shield against Hamas. Palestinians call it collective punishment for the enclave's 2 million residents, who suffer daily electricity cuts, bad drinking water and a collapsed economy. August 8, 2019.

In addition to all this, since the Oslo Accords of 1993 and 1995, which divided the West Bank into areas A (Palestinian control) B (Israeli Military control, Palestinian civil control) and C (Israeli control) and created the Palestinian Authority, Israel has created irreversible facts on the ground for the sake of its settlement project. By creating a segregated system of roads and closures, building the separation wall (parts of which run deep into the West Bank), and expanding settlements in strategic areas, Israel has rendered unattainable the territorial continuity of a future Palestinian state. The separation wall has created severe restrictions on the movement of Palestinians and has further reduced the land available to them. In Area C, which covers more than 60 percent of the West Bank, Israel retains nearly exclusive control, including of law enforcement, planning, and construction, 70 percent of Area C is included within the boundaries of Israeli settlements, and Palestinians use and development are heavily restricted in the remainder of the area.

Most resent attacks in August 2019 and also in July 2020, Muslims clash with Israeli police at Jerusalem holy site. The clashes came amid heightened tensions between Israel and the Palestinians, just days after an Israeli soldier was killed south of Jerusalem.

So the story goes in the St. Michaels Card, Thus he Michael the Archangel appears in Holy Scripture as the guardian of the children of Israel, their comfort and protector in times of sorrow or conflict.

Saint Michael the Archangel: Defend us in battle. Be our protection against the wickedness and snares of the devil. May God rebuke him, we humbly pray. O Prince of the heavenly hosts, by the power of God, thrust into hell Satan and all evil spirits who wander through the world for the ruin of souls Amen.

We also have Guardian Angels and the teaching about guardian angels is not a myth; certain groups of human beings do actually have personal angels. It was in recognition of this that, in speaking of the children of the heavenly kingdom, Jesus said in Matthew 18:10: "See that you do not despise one of these little ones, for I say to you that their angels in heaven always look upon the face of my heavenly Father."

Matthew 18:1, 4, At that time the disciples approached Jesus and said, "Who is the greatest in the kingdom of heaven?" He called a child over, placed it in their midst, and said, "Amen, I say to you, unless you turn and become like children, you will not enter the kingdom of heaven. And whoever receives one child such as this in my name receives me."

—— St Raphael an Archangel, angel. ——

There are many angels, In the book of Tobit, it explains what the angel of the Lord, Raphael did. What problems did the Archangel Raphael address in the book of Tobit? The book is primarily concerned with the problem of reconciling evil in the world with divine justice. Tobit and Sarah are pious

Jews unaccountably afflicted by malevolent forces, but their faith is finally rewarded, and God is vindicated as both just and omnipotent.

Due to his actions in the Book of Tobit and the Gospel of John, Saint Raphael is an accounted patron to travelers, the blind, happy meeting, nurses, physicians, medical workers, matchmakers, Christian marriage, and Catholic studies.

What is the message of the Book of Tobit?

Liturgical and religious significance doctrinally, the book is cited for its teaching on the intercession of angels, filial piety, and reverence for the dead. Tobit is also made reference to in chapter 5 of 1 Megabyan, a book considered canonical in the Ethiopian Orthodox Tewahedo Church.

Book of Tobit chapter 6:5, 9, The angel then told him, "Slit the fish open and take out its gall, heart, and liver, and keep them with you; but throw away the other entrails. Its gall, heart and liver are useful for medicine. After Tobiah had slit the fish open, he put aside the gall, heart and liver. Then he roasted and ate part of the fish; the rest he salted and kept for the journey.

Afterward the two of them traveled on together till they drew near to Media. Then the young man asked the angel this question: "Brother Azariah, what medicine is in the fish's heart, liver and gall?" He answered, "As for the fish's heart and liver, if you burn them to make smoke in the presence of a man or woman who is afflicted by a demon or evil spirit, any affliction will flee and never return. As for the gall, if you apply it to the eyes of one who has white scales, blowing right into them, sight will be restored.

St Gabriel an Archangel. In the Hebrew Bible. Gabriel appears to the prophet Daniel to explain his visions (Daniel 8:15-26, 9:21-27). The archangel appears in such other ancient Jewish writing as the Book of Enoch. Alongside Archangel Michael, Gabriel is described as a guardian angel of Israel, defending this people against the angels of the other nations. The Gospel of Luke relates the stories of the Annunciation, in which the Angel Gabriel appears to Zechariah and the Virgin Mary, foretelling the births of John the Baptist and Jesus, respectively (Luke 1:11-38). Many Christian traditions - including Anglicanism, Eastern Orthodoxy, and Roman Catholicism revere Gabriel as a Saint.

What are the 4 types of conflicts?
1) Conflicts with the self
2) Conflicts with others
3) Conflicts with the environment and
4) Conflict with the supernatural.

Ephesians 6:18, With all prayer and supplication, pray at every opportunity in the Spirit. To that end, be watchful with all perseverance and supplication for all the holy ones and also for me, that speech may be given me to open my mouth, to make known with boldness the mystery of the gospel for which I am an ambassador in chains, so that I may have the courage to speak as I must."

CHAPTER 5

It is he who prepares for their return from the Persian captivity.

Zion returnees) refers to the event in the biblical books of Ezra-Nehemiah in which the Jews returned to the Land of Israel from Babylonian exile following the decree by the Emperor Cyrus the Great, the conqueror of the Neo-Babylonian Empire in 539 B.C.E. also known as Cyrus's edict.

Zerubbabel, who led the first group of exiles back to Jerusalem The return to Zion, Initially, around 50,000 Jews made Aliyah to the land of Israel following the decree of Cyrus as described in Ezra, whereas most remained in Babylon.

I the second exodus from Babylon, How many Jews returned to Jerusalem with Ezra?

According to the account in the Book of Ezra, 42,360, not including servants or handmaids, made Aliyah in this wave to Jerusalem and Judah. Among them, there were 24,144 ordinary men (57.12%) and 12,452 women and children (29.46%)

The rebuilding of the Second Temple. The date is generally thought to have been between 538 and 520 B.C. Zerubbabel also laid the foundation of the Second Temple in Jerusalem soon after.

In the year 539 B.C.E. after uniting the Persian and Median Kingdoms under his rule, King Cyrus subdued the Babylonian Empire. In 538 B.C.E.

King Cyrus made a public declaration granting the Jews the right to return to Judah and rebuild the Temple in Jerusalem.

Why did Cyrus let the Jews return?

Cyrus allowed them to return to their promised land. The Jews praised the Persian emperor in scripture as a savior to whom God gave power over other kingdoms so that he would restore them to Jerusalem and allow them to rebuild their temple.

In Isaiah 45:1, 2, 3, Thus says the Lord to his anointed, Cyrus, who right hand I grasp, subduing nations before him, stripping kings of their strength, opening doors before him, leaving the gates unbarred: I will go before you and level the mountains; Bronze doors I will shatter, iron bars I will snap. I will give you treasures of darkness, riches hidden away. That you may know I am the Lord, the God of Israel, who calls you by name.

Before I go to the book of Jeremiah, which talks about the return of the Jews back to Jerusalem, we need to talk about the spiritual warfare that's going on in the heavenly places, that started in the book of Genesis chapter 3:1, Now the snake was the most cunning of all the wild animals that the Lord God had made.

So who is this serpent? In the Book of Revelation chapter 12:9, it reads: The huge dragon, the ancient serpent, who is called the Devil and Satan, who deceived the whole world, was thrown down to earth, and its angels were thrown down with it.

Revelation 12:7, 8, Explains what why it happened. It reads: Then war broke out in heaven; Michael and his angels battled against the dragon. The dragon and its angels fought back, but they did not prevail and there was no longer any place for them in heaven.

Now if you go back to Genesis 3:1, where it reads: Now the snake was the most cunning of all the wild animals that the Lord God had made. Let's see what it says about that in Genesis 1:31, God looked at everything he had made, and found it very good. Evening came, and morning followed— the sixth day. But really the knowledge of good and evil starts in:

Genesis 2:9, Knowledge of good and evil.
Genesis 3:1 Serpent already in the garden.
Genesis 3:3 That's why God said not to eat.

The Prophet Ezekiel reveals that Lucifer was that anointed cherub that covert. From Genesis 1:31 to Genesis chapter 3, Lucifer changes to the serpent (Satan) who tempts Adam and Eve.

In Ezekiel 28:11, 16, talks about this situation.

The word of the Lord came to me: Son of man, raise a lament over the king of Tyre, and say to him: Thus says the Lord God:

You were a seal of perfection,
    full of wisdom, perfect in beauty.
In Eden, the garden of God, you lived;
    precious stones of every kind were your covering:
Carnelian, topaz, and beryl,
    chrysolite, onyx, and jasper,
    sapphire, garnet, and emerald.
Their mounts and settings
    were wrought in gold,
    fashioned for you the day you were created.
With a cherub I placed you;
    I put you on the holy mountain of God,
    where you walked among fiery stones.
Blameless were you in your ways
    from the day you were created,
Until evil was found in you.
    your commerce was full of lawlessness, and you sinned.

Some propose that the King of Tyre was actually possessed by Lucifer, now Satan, making the link between the two even more powerful and applicable.

In Isaiah 14:12, "How you have fallen from the heavens, O Morning Star, son of the dawn! How you have been cut down to the earth, you who conquered nations!"

Jesus sees the same thing, in Luke 10:17, 20, The seventy-two returned rejoicing, and said, "Lord, even the demons are subject to us because of your name." Jesus said, "I have observed Satan fall like lightning from the sky. Behold, I have given you the power to tread upon serpents' and scorpions and upon the full force of the enemy and nothing will harm you. Nevertheless, do not rejoice because the spirits are subject to you, but rejoice because your names are written in heaven."

The people also ask, what was Satan's name when he was an angel? Lucifer was that anointed cherub.

Many Christians believe the Devil was once a beautiful angel named Lucifer who defied God and fell from grace. This assumption that he is a fallen angel is often based on the book of Isaiah 14:12 which says, "How you have fallen from the heavens, O Morning Star, son of the dawn! How you have been cut down to the earth, you who conquered nations!" And these Christians are right according to Ezekiel 28:11, 19, "The word of the Lord came to me: Son of man, raise a lament over the king of Tyre, and say to him: Thus says the Lord: You were a seal of perfection, full of wisdom, perfect in beauty. In Eden, the garden of God, you lived; precious stones of every kind were your covering: carnelian, topaz, and beryl, chrysolite, onyx, and jasper, sapphire, garnet and emerald. Their mounts and settings were wrought in gold, fashioned for you the day you were created. With a cherub I placed you; I put you on the holy mountain of God, where you walked among fiery stones. Blameless were you in your ways from the day you were created, until evil was found in you. Your commerce was full lawlessness, and you sinned. Therefore, I banished you from the mountain of God; the cherub drove you out from among the fiery stones. Your heart had grown haughty because of your beauty; you corrupted your wisdom because of your splendor. I cast you to the ground, I made you a spectacle in the sight of kings. Because of the enormity of your guilt, and the perversity of your trade, you defiled your sanctuary. I brought fire out of you; it devoured you; I made you ashes on the ground in the eyes of all who see you. All the nations who knew you are appalled on account of you; you have become a horror, never to be again.

Now this is what's going to happen to this fallen angels and the antichrist beast, and the false prophet. The book of Revelations, Chapters 19 and 20 will tell you about the end of these evil demons.

Revelations 19: 11, 19, Then I saw the heavens opened, and there was a white horse; its rider was called "Faithful and True." He judges and wages war in righteousness. His eyes were like a fiery flame, and one his head were many diadems. He had a name inscribed that no one knows except himself. He wore a cloak that had been dipped in blood, and his name was called the Word of God. The armies of heaven followed him, mounted on white horses and wearing clean white linen. Out of his mouth came a sharp sword to strike the nations. He will rule them with an iron rod, and he himself will tread out in the wine press the wine of the fury and wrath of God the almighty. He has a name written on his cloak and on his thigh, "King of kings and Lord of lords."

Then I saw an angel standing on the sun. He cried out in a loud voice to all the birds flying high overhead, "Come here. Gather for God's great feast, to eat the flesh of kings, the flesh of military officers, and the flesh of warriors, the flesh of horses and of their riders, and the flesh of all, free and slave, small and great." Then I saw the beast and the kings of the earth and their armies gathered to fight against the one riding the horse and against his army. The beast was caught and with it the false prophet who had performed in its sight the signs by which he led astray those who had accepted the mark of the beast and those who had worshipped its image.

This is John Michael Gurule and I must interject that this is the part that I enjoyed the most:

Revelations 19:20, The beast was caught and with it the false prophet who had performed in its sight the signs by which he led astray those who had accepted the mark of the beast and those who had worshiped its image. The two were both thrown alive into the fiery pool burning with sulfur.

Revelation 20, 1, 10, Then I saw an angel come down from heaven, holding in his hand the key to the abyss and a heavy chain. He seized the dragon, the ancient serpent, which is the Devil or Satan, and tied it up for a thousand years and threw it into the abyss, which he locked over it and sealed, so that it could no longer lead the nations astray until the thousand years are completed. After this, it is to be released for a short time.

Then I saw thrones; those who sat on them were entrusted with judgment. I also saw the souls of those who had been beheaded for their witness to Jesus and for the word of God, and who had not worshipped the beast or its image nor had accepted its mark on their foreheads or hands. They came to life and they reigned with Christ for a thousand years. The rest of the dead did not come to life until the thousand years were over. This is the first resurrection. Blessed and holy is the one who shares in the first resurrection. The second death has no power over these; they will be priests of God and of Christ, and they will reign with him for the thousand years,

When the thousand years are completed, Satan will be released from his prison. He will go out to deceive the nations at the four corners of the earth, Gog and Magog, to gather them for battle; their number is like the sand of the sea. They invaded he breadth of the earth and surrounded the camp of the holy ones and the beloved city. But fire came down from heaven and consumed them. The Devil who had led them astray was thrown into the pool of fire and sulfur, where the beast and the false prophet were. There they will be tormented day and night forever and ever.

This has not happened yet. But if you read Daniel chapters 10, 11, and 12. It goes like this, chapter 10 is about Spiritual Warfare, chapter 11, the description of the Anti-Christ and chapter 12, The Salvation of Israel, the modern state of Israel.

Before I go back to it, it is he who prepares for their return from the Persian captivity. I want to show you the modern day world, my name is John Michael Gurule, I'm 63 years old and the year is 2021, what happened in the book of Genesis chapter 3, the doctrine of the fall comes from a biblical interpretation. At first, Adam and Eve lived with God in the Garden of Eden, but the serpent tempted them into eating the fruit from the tree of knowledge of good and evil, which God had forbidden. That was the Fall of Man. Since temptation is something that Christians face and struggle against every day, it is necessary that we understand how it presents itself in our lives. We can gain much insight in the nature of temptation from the first temptation in Genesis 3:1-6.

The Temptation of Christ is a biblical narrative detailed in the Gospels of Matthew, Mark and Luke. After being baptized by John the Baptist, Jesus was tempted by the devil for 40 days and nights in the Judaean Desert. During this time, Satan came to Jesus and tried to tempt him. Jesus having refused each temptation, Satan then departed and Jesus returned to Galilee to begin his ministry. During this time entire time of spiritual battle, Jesus was fasting.

The writer of the Epistle to the Hebrews also refers to Jesus having been tempted in every way that we are, except without sin.

Mark's account is very brief, merely noting the event. Matthew and Luke describe the temptations by recounting the details of the conversations between Jesus and Satan. Since the elements that are in Matthew and Luke but not in Mark are mostly pairs of quotations rather than detailed narration, many scholars believe these extra details originate in the theoretical Q Document. The temptation of Christ is not explicitly mentioned in the Gospel of John but in this Gospel Jesus does refer to the Devil, the prince of this world," having no power over Him.

You can find the temptations of Jesus in Mark 4:1, 11, Matthew 4:1, 11, and Luke 4:1, 13.

The Oneness of God In Christ.

1 Timothy 2: 5, For there is one God. There is also one mediator between God and the human race, Christ Jesus, himself human, who gave himself as ransom for all.

Temptation and Sin

According to all four gospels, Jesus was brought to the "Place of a Skull" and crucified with two thieves, with the charge of claiming to be "King of the Jews", and the soldiers divided his clothes before he bowed his head and died.

What is the meaning of Jesus sacrifice?

Jesus came to give himself as a sacrifice for all people so that we could escape our corruption and reconnect with God. This plan was announced at the beginning of human history, such that even the ancient Chinese knew of it. It was signed by God in the sacrifice of Abraham by pointing to Mount Moriah where Jesus' sacrifice would be provided. Then the Jewish Passover sacrifice was a sign pointing to the day of the year when Jesus would be sacrificed. Further details were predicted in various prophecies in the Old Testament.

Why is his sacrifice so important? This is a question that summarizes the whole Bible, it is its main message. The Bible declares a law when it states:

"For the wages of sin is death, but the gift of God is eternal life in Christ Jesus our Lord." (Romans 6:23)

"Sin and Death" literally mean 'separation'. When our soul separates from our body we die physically. Similarly, we are even now separated from God spiritually. This is true because God is Holy (sinless) while we have become corrupted from our original creation and so we sin.

This can be pictured with two cliffs with God on the opposite side from us separated by a large gap. Just like a branch that has been cut from a tree is separated and dead, so we have cut ourselves off from God and become separated and spiritually dead.

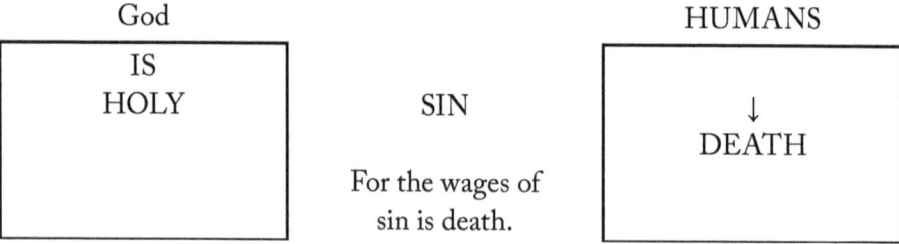

This separation causes guilt and fear. So what we naturally try to do is build bridges to take us from our side (of death) to God's side. We do this in many different ways: going to church, temple or mosque, being good, helping the poor, meditation, trying to be more helpful, praying more, etc. Put all that in here.

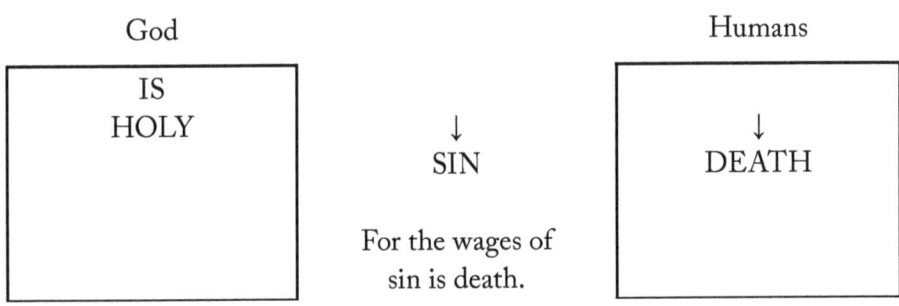

The problem is that our hard efforts, merits, and deeds, though not wrong, are insufficient because the payment required (the wages) for our sins is 'death'. Our efforts are like a 'bridge' that tries to cross the gap separating us from God - but in the end cannot do it. This is because good merit will not solve our root problem. It is like trying to heal cancer (which results in death) by eating a vegetarian diet. Eating vegetarian is not bad and it may even be good, but it will not cure cancer. For a cancer cure you need a totally different treatment.

This Law is Bad News. It is so bad we often do not even want to hear it and we fill our lives with activities and things hoping this law will go away. But the Bible stresses this law of sin and death to get our attention to focus on the cure that is simple and powerful.

"For the wages of sin is death but ..." (Romans 6:23)

The small word 'but' shows that the direction of the message is about to change directions, to the Good News of the Gospel - the cure. It shows both the goodness and love of God.

"For the wages of sin is death, but the gift of God is eternal life in Christ Jesus our Lord," Romans 6:23.

The good news of the gospel is that the sacrifice of Jesus' death is sufficient to bridge this separation between us and God. We know this because three days after his death Jesus rose bodily, coming alive again in a physical resurrection. Most of us do not know about the evidence for his resurrection. Jesus' sacrifice was prophetically acted out in Abraham's sacrifice and the Passover sacrifice. These signs pointing to Jesus were put there to help us find the cure.

Jesus said about himself: "Amen, amen, I say to you, before Abraham came to be, I AM." (John 8:58)

When Jesus said he was 'I AM', he was using an Old Testament name for God. But Jesus was also a man. As the Bible says:

"For there is one God. There is also one mediator between God and the human race, Christ Jesus, himself human, who gave himself as ransom for all." (1 Timothy 2:5)

Because he was both human and Divine, he is a mediator between God and mankind. Therefore, he can 'touch' both sides of the chasm and span the gap separating God and people. He is a bridge which can be pictured like the following:

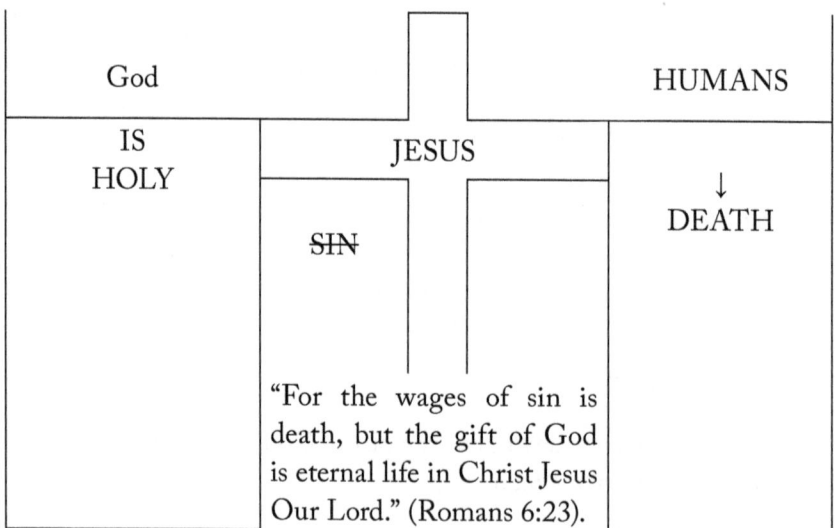

Galatians 1:3, 5,

"Grace to you and peace from God our Father and the Lord Jesus Christ, who gave himself for our sins that he might rescue us from the present evil age in accord with the will of our God and Father, to whom be glory forever and ever. Amen>"

Revelation 5:9, 10,

They sang a new hymn:

"Worthy are you to receive the scroll
    and to break open its seals,
For you were slain and with your
    blood you purchased for God
Those from every tribe and tongue,
    people and nation.
You made them a kingdom and priests for
    our God,
And they will reign on earth."

Death to Sin, Alive in Christ, we can choose to live in hell, or heaven. What is purgatory? We will learn more about that in this book.

We are going back to he who prepares for their return from the Persian captivity, but we do need to learn about all the key players in this story which comes from the Bible. And that we can find in Daniel chapter 10. After much research, I will give you all the names of everyone in Daniel chapter 10.

The first one is King Cyrus, verse one, In the third year of Cyrus King of Persia.

In Isaiah 45:1, 3,

Thus says the Lord to his anointed, Cyrus,
    whose right hand I grasp,
Subduing nations before him,
    stripping kings of their strength,
Opening doors before him,
    leaving the gates unbarred;

I will go before you
    and level the mountains;
Bronze doors I will shatter,
    iron bars I will snap.
I will give you treasures of darkness,
    riches hidden away,
That you may know I am the Lord,
    the God of Israel, who calls you by name.

The second person is the prophet Daniel. Daniel is the hero of the biblical book of Daniel. A noble Jewish youth Jerusalem who is taken into captivity by King Nebuchadnezzer of Babylon and required to serve the king.

In verse one Daniel chapter 10, a message was revealed to Daniel.

The third person, the divine Jesus Christ visits Daniel. (Daniel 10:2, 6)

Daniel 10:2, 6, In those days, I, Daniel, mourned three full weeks. I ate no savory food, took no meat or wine, and did not anoint myself at all until the end of the three weeks.

On the twenty-fourth day of the first month I was on the bank of the great river, the Tigris. As I looked up, I saw a man dressed in linen with a belt of find gold around his waist. His body was like chrysolite, his face shone like lightning, his eyes were like fiery torches, his arms and feet looked like burnished bronze, and the sound of his voice was like the roar of a multitude.

Daniel 10: 7, I alone, Daniel, saw the vision; but great fear seized those who were with me; they fled and hid themselves, although they did not see the vision.

In the book of Daniel chapter 10:2, 6 is the same Jesus Christ as in Revelation 1:10, 20. This is the revelation of Jesus Christ, I will start at verse 9.

Revelation 1:9-20, I, John, your brother, who share with you the distress, the kingdom, and the endurance we have in Jesus, found myself on the island called Patmos because I proclaimed God's word and gave testimony to Jesus. I was caught up in the spirit on the Lord's day and heard behind me a voice as loud as a trumpet, which said, "Write on a scroll what you see and send it to the seven churches: to Ephesus, Smyrna, Pergamum, Thyatira, Sardis, Philadelphia, and Laodicea." Then I turned to see whose voice it was that spoke to me, and when I turned, I saw seven gold lampstands and in the midst of the lampstands one like a son of man, wearing an ankle-length robe, with a gold sash around his chest. The hair of his head was as white as white wool or as snow, and his eyes were like a fiery flame. His feet were like polished brass refined in a furnace, and his voice was like the sound of rushing water. In his right hand he held seven stars. A sharp two-edge sword came out of his mouth, and his face shone like the sun at its brightest.

When I caught sight of him, I fell down at his feet as though dead. He touched me with his right hand and said, "Do not be afraid. I am the first and the last, the one who lives. Once I was dead, but now I am alive forever and ever. I hold the keys to death and the netherworld. Write down, therefore, what you have seen, and what is happening, and what will happen afterwards. t will happen afterwards. This is the secret meaning of the seven stars you saw in my right hand, and the seven gold lampstands: the seven stars are the angels of the seven churches, and the seven lampstands are the seven churches."

Revelation 19

The second coming kingdom of Jesus Christ.

This Jesus Christ in Revelation 19, is the same Jesus in the book of Daniel 3:23, 25, reads.

But these three fell, bound, into the midst of the white-hot furnace. They walked about in the flames, singing to God and blessing the Lord. Azariah stood up in the midst of the fire and prayed aloud.

Daniel 3:91, 92, Then King Nebuchadenezzar was startled and rose in haste, asking his counselors, "Do we not cast three men bound into the fire?" "Certainly, O king," they answered. "But, he replied, "I see four men unbound and unhurt, walking in the fire, and the fourth looks like a son of God." The same Jesus in Revelation 1:13, 15, and the same Jesus in Daniel 10:2, 6. In John 17:5 it reads, "Now glorify me, Father, with you, with the glory that I had with you before the world began." This is Jesus talking to God Almighty, his Father in heaven.

What is pre-incarnated Christ?

The pre-existence of Christ asserts the existence of Christ before his incarnation as Jesus. One of the relevant Bible passages is John 1:1-18.

John 1:18, No one has ever seen God, The only Son, God, who is at the Father's side, has revealed him."

Exodus 33:20, 23. But you cannot see my face, for no one can see me and live. Here, continued the Lord, is a place near me where you shall station yourself on the rock. When my glory passes I will set you in the cleft of the rock and will cover you with my hand until I have passed by. Then I will remove my hand, so that you may see my back; but my face may not be seen.

Deuteronomy 4:15, Because you saw no form at all on the day the Lord spoke to you at Horeb from the midst of the fire, be strictly on your guard.

1 Timothy 2:5, For there is one God. There is also one mediator between God and the human race, Christ Jesus, himself human.

1 Corinthians 11:3, But I want you to know that Christ is the head of every man, and a husband the head of the wife, and God the head of Christ.

Matthew 28:19, "Go, therefore, and make disciples of all nations, baptizing them in the name of the Father, and of the Son, and of the holy Spirit."

Mark 16:19, So then the Lord Jesus, after he spoke to them, was taken up into heaven and took his seat at the right hand of God.

What I'm doing is proving to you that the vision Daniel saw in Daniel 10:2, 6, and the vision that John saw in the Book of Revelation 1:12, 15, and in Revelation 19 are the same person Jesus Christ.

The Book of Revelation 1:1, 2, John is taken to heaven in the spirit, reads: The revelation of Jesus Christ, which God gave to him, to show his servants what must happen soon. He made it known by sending his angel to his servant John, who gives witness to the word reporting what he saw.

Revelation 19.

The second coming of the Kingdom of Jesus Christ and the defeat of the beast, anti-Christ, and the false prophet.

Revelation 19: 1-21. The defeat of Satan.

After this I heard what sounded like the loud voice of a great multitude in heaven, saying:

"Alleluia!
Salvation, glory, and might belong to our God,
     for true and just are his judgments.
He has condemned the great harlot
     who corrupted the earth with her harlotry.
He has avenged on her the blood of his servants."

They said a second time:

"Alleluia! Smoke will rise from her forever and ever."

The twenty-four elders and the four living creatures fell down and worshiped God who sat on the throne, saying, "Amen. Alleluia."

A voice coming from the throne said:

"Praise our God, all you his servants,
     And you who revere him, small and great."

Then I heard something like the sound of a great multitude or the sound of rushing water or mighty peals of thunder, as they said:

"Alleluia!
The Lord has established his reign,
    our God, the almighty.
Let us rejoice and be glad
    and give him glory.
For the wedding day of the Lamb has come,
    his bride has made herself ready.
She was allowed to wear
    a bright, clean linen garment."

(The linen represents the righteous deeds of the holy ones.)

Then the angel said to me, "Write this: Blessed are those who have been called to the wedding feast of the Lamb. And he said to me, "These words are true; they come from God." I fell at his feet to worship him. But he said to me, "Don't! I am a fellow servant of yours and of your brothers who bear witness to Jesus. Worship God. Witness to Jesus is the spirit of prophecy.

Then I saw the heavens opened, and there was a white horse; its rider was called "Faithful and True." He judges and wages war in righteousness. His eyes were like a fiery flame, and on his head were may diadems. He had a name inscribed that no one knows except himself. He wore a cloak that had been dipped in blood, and his name was called the Word of God. The armies of heaven followed him, mounted on white horses and wearing clean white linen. Out of his mouth came a sharp sword to strike the nations. He will rule them with an iron rod, and he himself will tread out in the wine press the wine of the fury and wrath of God the almighty. He has a name written on his cloak and on his thigh, "King of kings and Lord of lords."

Then I saw an angel standing on the sun. He cried out in a loud voice to all the birds flying high overhead, "Come here. Gather for God's greatest feast, to eat the flesh of kings, the flesh of military officers, and the flesh of warriors, the flesh of horses and of their riders, and the flesh of all, free and slave, small and great." Then I saw the beast and the kings of the earth and their armies gathered to fight against the one riding the horse and against his army. The beast was caught and with it the false prophet who had performed in its sight the signs by which led astray those who had accepted the mark of the beast and those who had worshiped its image. The two were thrown alive into the fiery pool burning with sulfur. The rest were killed by the sword that came out of the mouth of the one riding the horse, and all the birds gorged themselves on their flesh.

Revelation 20: 1-15, Then I saw an angel come down from heaven, holding in his hand the key to the abyss and a heavy chain. He seized the dragon, the ancient serpent, which is the Devil or Satan and tied it up for a thousand years and threw it into the abyss, which he locked over it and sealed, so that it could no longer lead the nations astray until the thousand years are completed. After this, it is to be released for a short time.

Then I saw thrones; those who sat on them were entrusted with judgment. I also saw the souls of those who had been beheaded for their witness to Jesus and for the word of God, and who had not worshiped the beast or its image nor had accepted its mark on their foreheads or hands. They came to life and they reigned with Christ for a thousand years. The rest of the dead did not come to life until the thousand years were over. This is the first resurrection. Blessed and holy is the one who shares in the first resurrection. The second death has no power over these; they will be priests of God and of Christ, and they will reign with him for the thousand years.

When the thousand years are completed, Satan will be released from his prison. He will go out to deceive the nations at the four corners of the earth, Gog and Magog, to gather them for battle; their number is like the sand of the sea. They invaded the breadth of the earth ad surrounded the camp of the holy ones and the beloved city. But fire came down from heaven and consumed them. The Devil who had led them astray was thrown into the pool of fire and sulfur, where the beast and the false prophet were. There they will be tormented day and night forever and ever.

Next I saw a large white throne and the one who was sitting on it. The earth and the sky fled from his presence and there was no place for them. I saw the dead, the great and the lowly, standing before the throne, and scrolls were opened. Then another scroll was opened, the book of life.

The dead were judged according to their deeds, by what was written in the scrolls. The sea gave up its dead; then Death and Hades gave up their dead. All the dead were judged according to their deeds. Then Death and Hades were thrown into the pool of fire. (This pool of fire is the second death.) Anyone whose name was not found written in the book of life was thrown into the pool of fire.

CHAPTER 6

The Angel Gabriel

The 4th Person mentioned in the Book of Daniel chapter 10.

What does the Bible say about the Angel Gabriel?

The angel Gabriel is an angel of God who is mentioned five times in the Holy Bible, when be brought messages from God to Daniel, Zechariah, and Mary the Mother of Jesus.

In Luke 1:19, And the angel said to him in reply, "I am Gabriel, who stands before God, I was sent to speak to you and to announce to you this good news."

The name Gabriel means – "God is my strength"

Gabriel Appears to Daniel 8: 15-16.

While I, Daniel, sought the meaning of the vision I had seen, one who looked like a man stood before me, and on the Ulai I heard a human voice that cried out, "Gabriel, explain the vision to this man."

Now if you go to the book of Exodus 3:1-6. It says that an angel of God, and God himself appeared to Moses as fire flaming out of a burning bush:

Exodus 3: 1-6, Meanwhile Moses was tending the flock of his father-in-law Jethro, the priest of Midian. Leading the flock beyond the wilderness, he came to the mountain of God, Horeb. There the angel of the Lord appeared to him as fire flaming out of a bush. When he looked, although the bush was on fire, it was not being consumed. So Moses decided, "I must turn aside to look at this remarkable sight. Why does the bush not burn up?" When the Lord saw that he had turned aside to look, God called out to him from the bush: Moses! Moses! He answered, "Here I am." God said: Do not come near! Remove your sandals from your feet, for the place where you stand is holy ground. I am the God of your father, he continued, the God of Abraham, the God of Isaac, and the God of Jacob. Moses hid his face for he was afraid to look at God.

I believe that it was God who talked to Gabriel and told him to make Daniel understand the vision."

The reason I bring up God talking to Moses, and also God talking to Gabriel, is that God has a super big part in the holy bible. And his Son Jesus Christ has a super big part in this holy bible. And all of the angels in heaven. Matthew 28: 18-19 reads: Then Jesus approached and said to them, "All power in heaven and on earth has been given to me. Go, therefore, and make disciples of all nations, baptizing them in the name of the Father, and of the Son, and of the holy Spirit." Amen and Amen.

Gabriel is first mentioned by name in Daniel 8:16. At this time, Daniel (of the lion's den fame) was living in Babylon where the Jews were in exile. As the book of Daniel records, though Daniel had been taken into exile into the service of the Babylonian king, he stayed true to his faith and gained great favor, becoming a powerful man who was also loyal to God.

Daniel had many visions of the future. It was after one such vision that the angel Gabriel visited him. Gabriel was called upon to explain the meaning of the vision to Daniel, illuminating what was to come. Gabriel returned at least two more times in Daniel 9:21, and Daniel 10:11-12.

Daniel 9:21-25, In this encounter, Gabriel pointed ahead to the "Anointed One," a name for the Messiah, who would be Jesus.

Gabriel Appears to Zechariah

The book of Luke, one of four Gospels, opens after a short introduction with the story of Zechariah, a priest. Luke records that Zechariah and his wife, Elizabeth, were righteous in the sight of God (Luke 1:16).

One day, as Zechariah went into the temple to burn incense before God, "an angel of the Lord appeared to him, standing at the right side of the altar of incense (Luke 1:11). This was Gabriel. Gabriel gave Zechariah the news that his wife, Elizabeth, would bear a son.

This seemed outlandish, as both were old and Elizabeth had been unable to have children, but Gabriel told Zechariah that he was to name the son John. Gabriel set out special directives for John and told Zechariah that John would bring back many to God and would prepare the way for the Lord - that "Lord" being Jesus, whose birth Gabriel would soon announce as well. The baby, John, was none other than John the Baptist, and he would be the one to baptize Jesus at the beginning of Jesus' ministry.

Luke 1:26-38, In the sixth month, the angel Gabriel was sent from God to a town of Galilee called Nazareth, to a virgin betrothed to a man named Joseph, of the house of David, and the virgin's name was Mary. And coming to her, he said, "Hail, favored one! The Lord is with you." But she was greatly troubled at what was said and pondered what sort of greeting this might be. Then the angel said to her, "Do not be afraid, Mary, for you have found favor with God. Behold, you will conceive in your womb and bear a son, and you shall name him Jesus. He will be great and will be called Son of the Most High, and the Lord God will give him the throne of David his father, and he will rule over the house of Jacob forever, and of his kingdom there will be no end." But Mary said to the angel, "How can this be, since I have no relations with a man?" And the angel said to her in reply, "The holy Spirit will come upon you and the power of the Most High will overshadow you. Therefore, the child to be born will be called holy, the Son of God. And behold, Elizabeth, your relative, has also conceived a son in her old age, and this is the sixth month for her who was called barren; for nothing will be impossible for God." Mary said, "Behold, I am the handmaid of the Lord. May it be done to me according to your word." Then the angel departed from her.

After this, the angel Gabriel left and he does not appear in the bible again, not by name.

Number Five person in Daniel chapter 10.

St Michael The Archangel, here are a number of verses on the Archangel St. Michael.

Jude 1:9, Yet the archangel Michael, when he argued with the devil in a dispute over the body of Moses, did not venture to pronounce a reviling judgment upon him but said, "May the Lord rebuke you!"

Revelation 12:7-9, Then war broke out in heaven; Michael and his angels battled against the dragon. The dragon and its angels fought back, but they did not prevail and there was no longer any place for them in heaven. The huge dragon, the ancient serpent, who is called the Devil and Satan, who deceived the whole world, was thrown down to earth, and its angels were thrown down with it.

Daniel 10:12, 13, Then he said to me, Do not be afraid, Daniel, for from the first day that you set your heart on understanding this and on humbling yourself before your God, your words were heard, and I have come in response to your words. But the prince of the kingdom of Persia was withstanding me for twenty-one days; then behold, Michael, one of the chief princes, came to help me, for I had been left there with the kings of Persia.

Daniel 12:1, "At that time there shall arise Michael, the great prince, guardian of your people; It shall be a time unsurpassed in distress since the nation began until that time. At that time your people shall escape, everyone who is found written in the book."

1 Thessalonians 4:16, For the Lord himself, with a word of command, with the voice of an archangel and with the trumpet of God, will come down from heaven, and the dead in Christ will rise first.

Daniel 10:21, "but I shall tell you what is written in the book of truth. No one supports me against these except Michael, your prince, and in the first year of Darius the Mede I stood to strengthen him and be his refuge.

The number six persons in Daniel chapter 10.

In Daniel chapter 10:18-21, The one who looked like a man touched me again and strengthened me, saying, "Do not fear, beloved. Peace! Take courage and be strong." When he spoke to me, I grew strong and said, "Speak, my lord, for you have strengthened me." "Do you know," he asked, why I have come to you? Soon I must fight the prince of Persia again. When I leave, the prince of Greece will come; but I shall tell you what is written in the book of truth. No on supports me against these except Michael, your prince, and in the first year of Darius the Mede I stood to strengthen him and be his refuge.

it reads Then again, the one having the likeness of a man touched me and strengthened me. And he said, O man greatly beloved fear not! Peace be to you; be strong, yes, be strong!" So, when he spoke to me I was strengthened and said, Let my Lord speak, for you have strengthened me.

Then, you have the verse that goes with this reading, its Revelation 12:7-8 and it reads: Then war broke out in heaven; Michael and his angels battled against the dragon. The dragon and its angels fought back, but they did not prevail and there was no longer an place for them in heaven.

Who are these princes, or principalities, that we as Christians war with?

Jesus said in John 14: 30 31, "I will no longer speak much with you, for the ruler of the world is coming. He has no power over me, but the world must know that I love the Father and that I do just as the Father has commanded me. Get up, let us go."

In Ephesians 2:1-2, You were dead in your transgressions and sins in which you once lived following the age of this world, following the ruler of the power of the air, the spirit that is now at work in the disobedient.

2 Corinthians 4:4, in whose case the god of this age has blinded the minds of the unbelievers, so that they may not see the light of the gospel of the glory of Christ, who is the image of God.

John 12:31, Now is the time of judgment on this world; now the ruler of this world will be driven out.

John 16:11, condemnation, because the ruler of this world has been condemned.

These are the five bible verses that say Satan is the prince of this world.

In chapter 10 in the book of Daniel, verse 20 reads, "Do you know", he asked, why I have come to you? Soon I must fight the prince of Persia again. When I leave, the prince of Greece will come."

Ephesians 6:10, 12, Explains what is going on here: Finally, draw your strength from the Lord and from his mighty power. Put on the armor of God so that you may be able to stand firm against the tactics of the devil. For our struggle is not with flesh and blood but with the principalities, with the powers, and the world rulers of this present darkness, with the evil spirits in the heavens.

So, what exactly are we dealing with here and are we in danger? I Peter 5:8 reads, Be sober and vigilant. Your opponent the devil is prowling around like a roaring lion looking for someone to devour.

John 10: 7, 10, So Jesus said again, "Amen, amen, I say to you, I am the gate for the sheep. All who came before me are thieves and robbers, but the sheep did not listen to them. I am the gate. Whoever enters through me will be saved and will come in and go out and find pasture. A thief comes only to steal and slaughter and destroy; I came so that they might have life and have it more abundantly."

There are many well-meaning "good" people who are actually buddying up with the devil. They join him and his demons on their playground. Evil has a field day with them and they are none the wiser. Ignorance however is not an excuse. You need to be aware of some of your actions.

By entertaining thoughts that are not in line with God's Word, you invite Satan's demons in to play on your playground. And your mind is the playground that he wants to wreak havoc in, Phil 4:8 says, Finally, brothers, whatever is true, whatever is honorable, whatever is just, whatever is pure, whatever is lovely, whatever is gracious, if there is any excellence and if there is anything worthy of praise, think about these things. That means that anything other than what is on this list has got to go - hatred, vengeance and self-pity are all access points to invite his demons in to play in your mind.

James 4:7, So submit yourselves to God. Resist the devil, and he will flee from you.

Ephesians 4:27, And do not leave room for the devil.

Revelation 12:12, 17, Therefore, rejoice, you heavens, and you who dwell in them. But woe to you, earth and sea, for the Devil has come down to you in great fury, for he knows he has but a short time.

When the dragon saw that it had been thrown down to the earth, it pursued the woman who had given birth to the male child. But the woman was given the two wings of the great eagle, so that she could fly to her place in the desert, where, far from the serpent, she was taken care of for a year, two years, and a half-year. The serpent, however, spewed a torrent of water out of his mouth after the woman to sweep her away with the current. But the earth helped the woman and opened its mouth and swallowed the flood that the dragon spewed out of its mouth. Then the dragon became angry with the woman and went off to wage war against the rest of her offspring, those who keep God's commandments and bear witness to Jesus. It took its position on the sand of the sea.

Revelation 13

Satan, the dragon, the first beast is the anti-Christ, and the false prophet. Here is that story.

1 John 2:18, Children, it is the last hour; and just as you heard that the antichrist was coming, so now many antichrists have appeared.

Satan, the prince of this world, commissioned the beast to persecute the church. This may be a reference to the popular legend that Nero would come back to life and rule again after his death which occurred in A.D. 68 from a self-inflicted stab wound in the throat; Domitian A.D. 81-96 embodied all the cruelty and impiety of Nero. Worshiped the beast: allusion to emperor worship, which Domitian insisted upon the ruthlessly enforced. Domitian, like Antiochus IV Epiphanes. In Daniel 7:8, they called this man Antiochus IV Epiphanes the little horn guy. He was anti-Christ, the verse reads: I was considering the ten horns it had, when suddenly another, a little horn, sprang out of their midst, and three of the previous horns were torn away to make room for it. This horn had eyes like human eyes, and a mouth that spoke arrogantly. In verses Daniel 7 21-22, For, as I watched, that horn made war against the holy ones and was victorious until the Ancient of Days came, and judgment was pronounced in favor of the holy ones of the Most High, and the time arrived for the holy ones to possess the kingship. You can find this story with this anti-Christ Antiochus IV Epiphanes starts in Daniel chapters 7 and 8, and this will take you to the first book of Maccabees. This Antiochus IV Epiphanes comes right after Alexander the Great, and his successors. Antiochus IV Epiphanes is the story of the first transgression of desolation. In Daniel 8:13, 14 it reads: I heard a holy one speaking, and another said to whichever one it was that spoke, "How long shall the events of this vision last concerning the daily sacrifice., the desolating sin." The giving over of the sanctuary and the host for trampling?" He answered him, "For two thousand three hundred evenings and mornings; then the sanctuary shall be set right." Add it up and it comes out to six and a half years. Antiochus IV Epiphanes, the first desolating is right here, is three years the first half. The second half is in Revelation 13:5, 8 which reads: The beast was given a mouth uttering proud boasts and blasphemies, and it was given authority to act for forty-two months. It opened its mouth to utter blasphemies against God, blaspheming his name and his dwelling and those who dwell in heaven. IT was also allowed to wage war against the holy ones and conquer them, and it was granted authority over every tribe, people, tongue, and nation. All the inhabitants of the earth will worship it, all whose names were not written from the foundation of the world in the book of life, which belongs to the Lamb who was slain. So, forty-two months and Antiochus IV Epiphanes three years. That's six and a half years. Antiochus IV Epiphanes desolating sin (167 to 164) persecuted the Jews in Jerusalem. Satan, Beast-anti-Christ, and false prophet, the last four-two months. You can read about Antiochus IV Epiphanes, in Catholic American Bible Society or the New Jerusalem Bible.

Domitian, like Antiochus IV Epiphanes both demand that they both be called by divine titles such as "our lord and god" and Jupiter. These people I mentioned are all anti-Christ, and there's more.

The two Beasts of Revelation 13

The first beast comes "out of the sea" and is given authority and power by the dragon. This first beast is initially mentioned in Revelation 11:7 as coming out of the abyss. His appearance is described in detail in Revelation 13:1-10 and some of the mystery behind his appearance is revealed in Revelation 17:7-8.

The second beast comes "out of the earth" and directs all people of the earth to worship the first beast. The second is associated with Revelation 13:11, 18 the false prophet.

The two beasts are aligned with the dragon in opposition to God. They persecute the "Saints" and those who do "not worship the beast (of the sea)" and influence the kings of the earth to gather for the battle of Armageddon. The two beasts are defeated by Christ and are thrown into the lake of fire mentioned in Revelation 19:18, 20.

Here is that story Revelation 13.

Remember we are still in Daniel 10 and these are the principalities, evil powers, and rulers of darkness.

Satan and his fallen followers are number 6, on the list in Daniel, I've heard many stories on who everyone is in Daniel 10. So, God's story would be number seven which is God's favorite number.

777 in the bible, Christianity. According to the American publication, the Orthodox Study Bible, 777 represents the threefold perfection of the

Trinity. The number 777, as triple 7, can be contrasted against triple 6, for the number of the Beast as 666.

As I was working on Daniel 10, it just worked out this way.

Matthew 5:48, So be perfect, just as your heavenly Father is perfect.

Matthew 28:19, Go, therefore, and make disciples of all nations, baptizing them n the name of the Father, and of the Son, and of the holy Spirit.

I'm John Michael Gurule, I am a Christian that goes to Catholic church. We read the Apostle's Creed all the time. It reads:

I believe in God, the Father Almighty, Creator of heaven and earth; and in Jesus Christ, His only Son, our Lord; who was conceived by the Holy Spirit, born of the Virgin Mary, suffered under Pontius Pilate, was crucified, died, and was buried. He descended into Hell; the third day He arose again from the dead. He ascended into heaven, sits at the right hand of God, the Father Almighty; from thence He shall come to judge the living and the dead.

I believe in the Holy Catholic Church, the communion of Saints, the forgiveness of sins, the resurrection of the body, and life everlasting. Amen.

Catholics are the true Christians. What defines a Catholic? A person who belongs to the Universal Christian Church. In 1 Corinthians 6:19-20, it reads: Do you not know that your body is a temple of the Holy Spirit within you, whom you have from God and that you are not your own? For you have been purchased at a price. Therefore, glorify God in your body.

I've heard people say, is the Holy Spirit a person? Yes, it is. That person is you, you are the temple of God, and of the Holy Spirit, there are three persons in the Trinity. The Apostles Creed Prayer, Amen. The Father God Almighty, God's Son Jesus Christ, and the believer in Jesus Christ, and the follower who obeys God.

Revelation 13: 1-18, Satan, and the two Beasts

Then I saw the beast come out of the sea with ten horns and seven heads; on its horns were ten diadems, and on its heads, blasphemous name(s). The beast I saw was like a leopard, but had feet like a bear's, and its mouth was like the mouth of a lion. To it the dragon gave its own power and throne, along with great authority. I saw that one of its heads seemed to have been mortally wounded, but this mortal wound was healed. Fascinated, the whole world followed after the beast and said, "Who can compare with the beast or who can fight against it?"

The beast was given a mouth uttering proud boasts and blasphemies, and it was given authority to act for forty-two months. It opened its mouth to utter blasphemies against God, blaspheming his name and his dwelling and those who dwell in heaven. It was also allowed to wage war against the holy ones and conquer them, and it was granted authority over every tribe, people, tongue, and nation. All the inhabitants of the earth will worship it, all whose names were not written from the foundation of the world in the book of life, which belongs to the Lamb who was slain.

Whoever has ears ought to hear these
    words.
Anyone destined for captivity goes into
    captivity.
Anyone destined to be slain by the sword
    shall be slain by the sword.

Such is the faithful endurance of the holy ones.

Then I saw another beast coming up out of the earth; it had two horns like a lamb's but spoke like a dragon. It wielded all the authority of the first beast in its sight and made the earth and its inhabitants worship the first beast, whose mortal wound had been healed. IT performed great signs, even making fire come down from heaven to earth in the sight of everyone. It deceived the inhabitants of the earth with the signs it was allowed to perform in the sight of the first beast who had been wounded by the sword and revived. It was then permitted to breathe life into the beast's image, so that the beast's image could speak and could have anyone who did not worship it put to death. It forced all the people; small and great, rich and poor, free and slave, to be given a stamped image on their right hands or their foreheads, so that no one could buy or sell except one who had the stamped image of the beast's name or the number that stood for its name.

Here is wisdom. Let him who has understanding calculate the number of the beast, for it is the number of a man: His number is 666.

The seventh person in Daniel 10 is God Almighty, the reason is the number seven is the number of completeness and perfection (both physical and spiritual). It derives much of its meaning from being tied directly to God's creation of all things.

In Matthew 5:48, So be perfect, just as your heavenly Father is perfect.

For example, Joshua 6:1, 17, Now Jericho was in a state of siege because of the presence of the Israelites. No one left or entered. And to Joshua the Lord said: I have delivered Jericho, its king, and its warriors into your power. Have all the soldiers circle the city, marching once around it. Do this for six days, with seven priests carrying ram's horns ahead of the ark. One the seventh day march around the city seven times, and have the priests blow the horns. When they give a long blast on the ram's horns and you hear the sound of the horn, all the people shall shout aloud. The wall of the city will collapse, and the people shall attack straight ahead.

Summoning the priests, Joseph, son of Nun, said to them, "Take up the ark of the covenant with seven of the priests carrying ram's horns in front of the ark of the Lord." And he ordered the people, "Proceed and surround the city, with the picked troops marching ahead of the ark of the Lord." When Joshua spoke to the people, the seven priests who carried the ram's horns before the Lord marched and blew their horns, and the ark of the covenant of the Lord followed them. In front of the priests with the horns marched the picked troops; the rear guard followed the ark, and the blowing of horns was kept up continually as they marched. But Joshua had commanded the people, "Do not shout or make any noise or outcry until I tell you, 'Shout!' Then you must shout. So, he had the ark of the Lord circle the city, going once around it, after which they returned to camp for the night.

Early the next morning, Joshua had the priests take up the ark of the Lord. The seven priests bearing the ram's horns marched in front of the ark of the Lord, blowing their horns. Ahead of these marched the picked troops, while the rear guard followed the ark of the Lord, and the blowing of horns was kept up continually. On this second day they again marched around the city once before returning to camp; and for six days in all they did the same.

On the seventh day, beginning at daybreak, they marched around the city seven times in the same manner; on that day only did they march around the city seven times. The seventh time around, the priests blew the horns and Joshua said to the people, "Now shout, for the Lord has given you the city. The city and everything in it is under the ban. Only Rahab the prostitute and all who are in the house with her are to live, because she hid the messengers we sent.

We are still in Daniel chapter 10, God is the seventh person. I believe that the third heaven, (the holy of holies), was giving us a message. This is a reminder that something went horribly wrong, referring to Lucifer (now Satan), as God's plan for Lucifer went horribly wrong. God says in Ezekiel 28:19, reads: All the nations who knew you are appalled on account of you; you have become a horror, never to be again.

CHAPTER 7

Genesis 1, 2, 3

In the book of Genesis, chapters 1, 2, 3, is where God's plan changed. It started off pretty good in chapter one, and two, then in chapter three, Lucifer decides to rebel against God, and he becomes Satan the tempter. This is where the horror begins.

In Isaiah 14:12, How you have fallen from heavens, O morning star, son of the dawn! How you have been cut down to earth, you who conquered nations!"

In 2 Timothy 3:16, All scripture is inspired by God and is useful for teaching, for refutation, for correction, and for training in righteousness, so that one who belongs to God may be competent, equipped for every good work.

Now I'm going to explain Genesis chapters one, two and three. In the creation of the world, God saw all he had made, and indeed it was very good. Evening came and morning came: the sixth day. In chapter two of Genesis, verse nine. This is where Lucifer shows up. Ezekiel 28:12, 14. You were a seal of perfection, full of wisdom, perfect in beauty. In Eden, the garden of God, you lived; precious stones of every kind were your covering: carnelian, topaz, and beryl, chrysolite, onyx, and jasper, sapphire, garnet, and emerald. Their mounts and settings were wrought in gold, fashioned for you the day you were created. With a cherub I placed you; I put you on the holy mountain of God, where you walked among fiery stones.

So, you can see Lucifer was created by God, and was there in the garden of Eden. In verse 15 of Ezekiel 28 it reads: blameless were you in your ways from the day you were create, until evil was found in you.

In Genesis 2:8, 9, The Lord God planted a garden in Eden, in the east, and placed there the man whom he had formed. Out of the ground the Lord God made grow every tree that was delightful to look at and good for food, with the tree of life in the middle of the garden and the tree of all knowledge of good and evil.

This is where Lucifer the anointed cherub, the first angel created, decides this is not what he wants, it looks like Lucifer wants more.

So, this is where Lucifer changes into Satan. Reason he wanted more than what he had. So, in Genesis chapter one, two, and three will explain why we have evil in the world. You will read these chapters in this book next.

Satan's plan now, is to kill, steal, and destroy you, and everybody around you. In John 10:10, also Jesus said, "A thief comes only to steal and slaughter and destroy; I came so that they might have life and have it more abundantly."

The first Book of Moses is called Genesis. The first part of Genesis focuses on the beginning and spread of sin in the world and culminates in the devastating flood in the days of Noah. The second part of the book focuses on God's dealings with one man, Abraham, through whom God promises to bring salvation and blessing to the world. Abraham and his descendants learn firsthand that it is always safe to trust the Lord in times of famine and feasting, blessing and bondage. From Abraham ... to Isaac ... to Jacob ... to Joseph ... God's promises begin to come to fruition in a great nation possessing great land.

Genesis Chapter 1: 1-30, Creation.

In the beginning, when God created the heavens and the earth—and the earth was without form or shape, with darkness over the abyss and a mighty wind sweeping over the waters—

Then God said: Let there be light, and there was light. God saw that the light was good. God then separated the light from the darkness. God called the light "day" and the darkness he called "night". Evening came, and morning followed—the first day.

Then God said: Let there be a dome in the middle of the waters, to separate one body of water from the other. God made the dome, and it separated the water below the dome from the water above the dome. And so it happened. God called the dome "sky". Evening came, and morning followed—the second day.

Then God said: Let the water under the sky be gathered into a single basin, so that the dry land may appear. And so it happened: the water under the sky was gathered into its basin, and the dry land appeared. God called the dry land "earth" and the basin of water he called "sea." God saw that it was good. Then God said: Let the earth bring forth vegetation: every kind of plant that bears seed and every kind of fruit tree on earth that bears fruit with its seed in it. And so it happened: the earth brought forth vegetation: every kind of plant that bears seed and every kind of fruit tree that bears fruit with its seed in it. God saw that it was good. Evening came, and morning followed—the third day.

Then God said: Let there be lights in the dome of the sky, to separate day from night. Let them mark the seasons, the days and the years, and serve as lights in the dome of the sky, to illuminate the earth. And so it happened: God make the two great lights, the greater one to govern the day, and the lesser one to govern the night, and the stars. God set them in the dome of the sky, to illuminate the earth, to govern the day and the night, and to separate the light from the darkness. God saw that it was good. Evening came, and morning followed—the fourth day.

Then God said: Let the water teem with an abundance of living creatures, and on the earth let birds fly beneath the dome of the sky. God created the great sea monsters and all kinds of crawling living creatures with which the water teems, and all kinds of winged birds. God saw that it was good, and God blessed them, saying: Be fertile, multiply, and fill the water of the seas; and let the birds multiply on the earth. Evening came, and morning followed—the fifth day.

Then God said: Let the earth bring forth every kind of living creature: tame animals, crawling things, and every kind of wild animal. And so it happened: God made every kind of wild animal, every kind of tame animal, and every kind of thing that crawls on the ground. God saw that it was good. Then God said: Let us make human beings in our image, after our likeness. Let them have dominion over the fish of the sea, the birds of the air, the tame animals, all the wild animals, and all the creatures that crawl on the earth.

God created mankind in his image; in the image of God he created them; male and female he created them.

God blessed them and God said to them: Be fertile and multiply; fill the earth and subdue it. Have dominion over the fish of the sea, the birds of the air, and all the living things that crawl on the earth. God also said: See, I give you every seed-bearing plant on all the earth and every tree that has seed-bearing fruit on it to be your food; and to all the wild animals, all the birds of the air, and all the living creatures that crawl on the earth, I give all the green plants for food. And so it happened. God looked at everything he had made, and found it very good. Evening came, and morning followed—the sixth day.

That was chapter one of Genesis, before I go to Genesis chapter two, I want to learn more and get a better understanding of God. From Genesis to the book of Revelation, and the seven extra books in the Catholic bible, to me this bible is like pure gold. The Bible is a precious book that fills the need of every soul. The messages found in it provide spiritual nourishment. There are chapters exactly suited for your particular need or iniquity.

God's message to man is expressed in different ways in various chapters of the Bible. There is much knowledge of God and the history of His people to be found in Genesis and other Old Testament chapters. The psalms and many New Testament chapters can be read as a source of real spiritual inspiration. Many teachings of Jesus such as Matthew 5, 6, and 7, as well as writing of the Apostles, give direction for our daily lives. It all combines to provide an understanding of God, His will for us, and His promises.

God has warmed the hearts of many readers as they have drawn from these blessed resources. Let us be encouraged to read these chapters. Let us read them not only to make ourselves feel better, but to let the message of God touch the need of our inner self.

As we continue in chapter two of Genesis, God will talk about Lucifer changing into Satan in verse nine, in which we will read right now. God knew right away when this change took place. The first created angel rebelled against God.

Genesis, Chapter 2: 1-25, Creation of Man and Woman

Then the heavens and the earth and all their array were completed. On the seventh day God completed the work he had been doing; he rested on the seventh day from all the work he had undertaken. God blessed the seventh day and made it holy, because on it he rested from all the work he had done in creation.

This is the story of the heavens and the earth at their creation. When the Lord God made the earth and the heavens—there was no field shrub on earth and no grass of the field had sprouted, for the Lord God had sent no rain upon the earth and there was no man to till the ground, but a stream was welling up out of the earth and watering all the surface of the ground—then the Lord God formed the man out of the dust of the ground and blew into his nostrils the breath of life, and the man became a living being.

The Lord God planted a garden in Eden, in the east, and placed there the man whom he had formed. Out of the ground the Lord God made grow every tree that was delightful to look at and good for food, with the tree of life in the middle of the garden and the tree of knowledge of good and evil.

A river rises in Eden to water the garden; beyond there it divides and becomes four branches. The name of the first is the Pishon; it is the one that winds through the whole land of Havilah, where there is gold. The gold of that land is good; bdellium and lapis lazuli are also there. The name of the second river is the Gihon; it is the one that winds all through the land of Cush. The name of the third river is the Tigris; it is the one that flows east of Asshur. The fourth river is the Euphrates.

The Lord God then took the man and settled him in the garden of Eden, to cultivate and care for it. The Lord God gave the man this order: You are free to eat from any of the trees of the garden except the tree of knowledge of good and evil. From that tree you shall not eat; when you eat from it you shall die.

The Lord God said: It is not good for the man to be alone. I will make a helper suited for him. So the Lord God formed out of the ground all the wild animals and all the birds of the air, and he brought them to the man to see what he would call them; whatever the man called each living creature was then its name. The man gave names to all the tame animals, all the birds of the air, and all the wild animals; but none proved to be a helper suited to the man.

So, the Lord God cast a deep sleep on the man, and while he was asleep, he took out one of his ribs and closed up its place with flesh. The Lord God then built the rib that he had taken from the man into a woman. When he brought her to the man, the man said:

> "This one, at last, is bone of my bones
> And flesh of my flesh;
> This one shall be called 'woman',
> For out of man this one has been taken.

That is why a man leaves his father and mother and clings to his wife, and the two of them become one body.

The man and his wife were both naked, yet they felt no shame.

Before we get into Genesis chapter three. The fall of man, woman, and Lucifer now Satan. We are still learning the mind of God.

We need to continue to read our bibles. For it contains the mind of God, the state of man, the way of salvation, doom of sinners and happiness of believers. Its doctrines are holy, its precepts are binding, its histories are true, and its decisions are immutable.

Read it to be wise, believe it to be safe, and practice it to be holy. It contains light to direct you, food to support you and comfort to cheer you. It is the traveler's map, the pilgrim's staff, the pilot's compass, the soldier's sword and the Christian's chapter.

Here paradise is restored, heaven opened, and the gates of hell disclosed. Christ is its grand subject, our good its design, and the glory of God its end. It should fill the memory, rule the heart, and guide the feet.

Read it slowly, frequently, prayerfully. It is a mine of wealth, a paradise of glory, and a river of pleasure. It is given you in life, will be open at the judgment and be remembered forever. It involves the highest responsibility, rewards the greatest labor and condemns all who trifle with its holy contents.

Genesis chapter three

The fall of Satan, and each of the three punishments, the snake, meaning Satan, the woman, the man, has a double aspect, one affecting the individual and the other affecting a basic relationship. The snake previously stood upright, enjoyed a reputation for being shrewder than other creatures, and could converse with human beings. The snake, Satan, must now move on its belly, and is more cursed than any creature, and inspires revulsion in human beings.

Expulsion from Eden, Chapter 3, 1-24, Now the snake was the most cunning of all the wild animals that the Lord God had made. He asked the woman, "Did God really say, 'You shall not eat from any of the trees in the garden'? The woman answered the snake: "We may eat of the fruit of the trees in the garden; it is only about the fruit of the tree I the middle of the garden that God said, 'You shall not eat it or even touch it, or else you will die.' But the snake said to the woman: 'You certainly will not die! God knows well that when you eat of it your eyes will be opened and you will be like gods, who know good and evil' The woman saw that the tree was good for good and pleasure to the eyes, and the tree was desirable for gaining wisdom. So she took some of its fruits and ate it; and she also gave some to her husband, who was with her, and he ate it. Then the eyes of both of them were opened, and they knew that they were naked; so, they sewed fig leaves together and made loincloths for themselves.

When they heard sound of the Lord God walking about in the garden at the breezy ime of the day, the man and his wife hid themselves from the Lord God among the trees of the garden. The Lord God then called to the man and asked him: Where are you? He answered,

"I heard you in the garden; but I was afraid, because I was naked, so I hid." Then God asked: Who told you that you were naked? Have you eaten from the tree of which I had forbidden you to eat? The man replied, "The woman whom you put here with me—she gave me fruit from the tree, so I ate it." The Lord God then asked the woman: What is this you have done? The woman answered, "The snake tricked me, so I age it."

Then the Lord said to the snake:

Because you have done this,
    cursed are you
    among all the animals, tame or wild;
On your belly you shall crawl,
    and dust you shall eat
    all the days of your life.
I will put enmity between you and the
        woman.
    and between your offspring and hers;
They will strike at your head,
    while you strike at their heel.

To the woman he said:

I will intensify your toil in childbearing;
    in pain you shall bring forth
        children.
Yet your urge shall be for your husband,
    and he shall rule over you.

To the man he said: Because you listened to your wife and ate from the tree about which I commanded you, you shall not eat from it,

Cursed is the ground because of you!
    in toil you shall eat its yield
    all the days of your life.
Thorns and thistles it shall bear for you,
    and you shall ear the grass of the field.
By the sweat of your brow
    you shall eat bread,
Until you return to the ground,
    from which you were taken;
For you are dust,
    and to dust you shall return.

The man gave his wife the name of "Eve", because she was the mother of all the living.

The Lord God made for the man and his wife garments of skin, with which he clothed them. The Lord God said: See! The man has become like one of us, know good and evil! Now, what if he also reaches out his hand to take fruit from the tree of life and eats of it and lives forever. The Lord God therefore banished him from the garden of Eden, to till the ground from which he had been taken. He expelled the man, stationing the cherubim and the fiery revolving sword east of the garden of Eden, to guard the way to the tree of life.

So Adam and Eve were driven out of the garden of Eden. In the book of Genesis 2:9, is where Lucifer changes into Satan. In Isaiah 14:12, 15, explains what happens to Lucifer, now Satan.

How you have fallen from the heavens, O Morning Star, son of the dawn! How you have been cut down to the earth, you who conquered nations! In your heart you said: I will scale the heavens; Above the stars of God I will set up my throne; I will take my seat on the Mount of Assembly, on the heights of Zaphon. I will ascend above the tops of the clouds; I will be like the Most High! No! Down to Sheol you will be brought to the depths of the pit!

Sheol, an underworld where souls of the dead went after the body died. The Greeks had one known as Hades.

Sheol in Hebrew means; the abode of the dead or of departed spirits. (lowercase) hell.

Hades, according to various Christian denominations, is the place or state of departed spirits, also known as Hell, borrowing the name of the Greek God of the dead.

Hades is the god of the underworld in Greek mythology. His realm is called, well, the underworld. Hades, Hell encompasses the entire underworld, whereas Tartarus is just one section - specifically, the place reserved for the unjust and wicked.

Tartarus, the infernal regions of ancient mythology. The name was originally used for the deepest region of the world, the lower of the two parts of the underworld.

Dudael is also implied to be the prison of all the fallen angels, especially the evil watchers, the entrance of which is located to the east of Jerusalem. The way this place is described, Dudael is sometimes considered as a region of the underworld, comparable to Tartarus or Gehenna.

CHAPTER 8

1 Peter 3:18, 22, The spirits in prison are the fallen angels.

The resurrection and the descent in hell.

For Christ also suffered for sins once, the righteous for the sake of the unrighteous, that he might lead you to God. Put to death in the flesh, he was brought to life in the spirit. In it he also went to preach to the spirits in prison, who had once been disobedient while God patiently waited in the days of Noah during the building of the ark, in which a few persons, eight in all, were saved through water. This prefigured baptism, which saves you now. It is not a removal of dirt from the body but an appeal to God for a clear conscience, through the resurrection of Jesus Christ, who has gone into heaven and is the right hand of God, with angels, authorities, and powers subject to him.

The spirits in prison are angels, support for the understanding that the spirits in prison are angelic being and not people is thought to be confirmed by 2 Peter 2:4, 5 and Jude 6 which refer to rebellious angels, punished by God with imprisonment. Just like 1 Peter 3:18, 22.

2 Peter 2:4, 5, Lessons of the past.

For if God did not spare the angels when they sinned, but condemned them to the chains of Tartarus and handed them over to be kept for judgment; and if he did not spare the ancient world, even though he preserved Noah, a herald of righteousness, together with seven others, when he brought flood upon the godless world.

Jude 1:6, The False Teachers; the certainty of punishment.

Verse 6, The angels too, who did not keep to their own domain but deserted their proper dwelling, he has kept in eternal chains, in gloom, for the judgment of the great day.

Matthew 25:31, 46, When the Son of Man comes in his glory, and all the angels with him, he will sit upon his glorious throne, and all the nations will be assembled before him.

What is the moral of the parable of the sheep and goats?

The Parable of the Sheep and Goats is found in Matthew 25:31, 46. In this parable Jesus uses the example of a shepherd who separates his sheep from his goats in order to help his followers understand what judgement will be like, here is that reading.

The Last Judgment

When the Son of Man comes in his glory, and all the angels with him, he will sit upon his glorious throne, and all the nations will be assembled before him. And he will separate them one from another, as a shepherd separates the sheet from the goats. He will place the sheep on his right and the goats on his left. Then the king will say to those on his right, Come, you who are blessed by my Father. Inherit the kingdom prepared for you from the foundation of the world. For I was hungry and you gave me food. I was thirsty and you gave me drink, a stranger and you welcomed me, naked and you clothed me, ill and you cared for me, in prison and you visited me. Then the righteous will answer him and say, 'Lord, when did we see you hungry and feed you, or thirsty and give you drink? When did we see you a stranger and welcome you, or naked and clothe you? When did we see you ill or in prison, and visit you? And the king will say to them in reply, Amen, I say to you, whatever you did for one of these least brothers of mine, you did it for me. Then he will say to those on his left,

Depart from me, you accurse, into the eternal fire prepared for the devil and his angels. I was thirsty and you gave me no drink, a stranger and you gave me no welcome, naked and you gave me no clothing, ill and in prison, and you did not care for me. Then they will answer and say, 'Lord, when did we see you hungry or thirsty or a stranger or naked or ill or in prison, and not minister to your needs? He will answer them, Amen, I say to you, what you did not do for one of these least ones, you did not do for me. And these will go off to eternal punishment, but the righteous to eternal life.

Who tempted Lucifer, an anointed cherub, who covers?

In Ezekiel 28:12, 16, You were a seal of perfection, full of wisdom, perfect in beauty. In Eden, the garden of God, you lived; precious stones of every kind were your covering: carnelian, topaz, and beryl, chrysolite, onyx, and jasper, sapphire, garnet, and emerald. Their mounts and settings were wrought in gold, fashioned for you the day you were created. With a cherub I placed you; I put you on the holy mountain of God, where you walked among fiery stones. Blameless were you in your ways from the day you were created, until evil was found in you. Your commerce was full of lawlessness, and you sinned. Therefore I banished you from the mountain of God; the cherub drove you out from among the fiery stones.

This was Lucifer being cast out of heaven, Lucifer's name changes to Satan.

Revelation 12:7, 9, Then war broke out in heaven; Michael and his angels battled against the dragon. The dragon and its angels fought back, but they did not prevail and there was no longer any place for them in heaven. The huge dragon, the ancient serpent, who is called the Devil or Satan, who deceived the whole world, was thrown down to earth, and its angels were thrown down with it.

Satan's fall from heaven is symbolically described in Isaiah 14:12, 14 and Ezekiel 28:12-18. While these two passages are referring specifically to the kings of Babylon and Tyre, they also reference the spiritual power behind those kings, namely, Satan. These passages describe why Satan fell, but they do not specifically say when the fall occurred. What we do know is this: the angels were created before the earth. In Job 38:4, 7, God talks to Job,

Where were you when I founded the earth? Tell me, if you have understanding. Who determined its size? Surely you know? Who stretched out the measuring line for it? Into what were its pedestals sunk, and who laid its cornerstone, while the morning stars sang together and the sons of God shouted for joy? Remember in Genesis 1:31, Then God looked at everything he had made, and found it very good. Evening came, and morning followed—the sixth day.

Lucifer was still the anointed cherub who covers; Ezekiel 28:14, 15 – reads: With a cherub I placed you; I put you on the holy mountains of God, where you walked among fiery stones. Blameless were you in your ways from the day you were created, until evil was found in you.

The first sign that Lucifer fell, and became Satan was in Genesis 2:9, reads: Out of the ground the Lord God made grow every tree that was delightful to look at and good for food, with the tree of life in the middle of the garden and the tree of the knowledge of good and evil.

Lucifer fell and became Satan before he tempted Adam and Eve in the Garden, Genesis 3:1, 14. Lucifer's fall, therefore, must have occurred somewhere after the time the angels were created and before he tempted Adam and Eve in the Garden of Eden. Lucifer's fall occurred a few minutes, hours, or days before he tempted Adam and Eve in the Garden.

Lucifer, now Satan. The book of Job tells us, at least at that time, Satan still had access to heaven and to the throne of God. One day when the sons of God came to present themselves before the Lord, the satan also came with them. The Lord said to the satan, "where have you come from?" Then the satan answered the Lord and said, "roaming the earth and patrolling it." Job 1:6, 7.

Apparently at that time, Satan was still moving freely between heaven and earth, speaking to God directly and answering for his activities.

At what point God discontinued this access is unknown.

Why did Lucifer fall from heaven? Lucifer fell because of pride. He desired to be God, not to be a servant of God. Notice the many "I will ..."

statements in Isaiah 14:12, 15. Ezekiel 28:12, 15 describes Lucifer as an exceedingly beautiful angel. Lucifer was an anointed cherub who covers, the most beautiful of all of God's creations, but he was not content in his position. Instead, Lucifer desired to be God, to essentially "kick God off his throne" and take over the rule of the universe. Satan wanted to be God, and interestingly enough, that is what Satan tempted Adam and Eve with in the Garden of Eden. Genesis 3:4, 5; reads: But the snake said to the woman: "You certainly will not die! God knows well that when you eat of it your eyes will be opened and you will be like gods, who know good and evil.

So how did Satan fall from heaven? Actually, a fall is not an accurate description. It would be far more accurate to say God cast Satan out of heaven, Isaiah 14:15; Ezekiel 28:16, 17. Satan did not fall from heaven; rather, Satan was pushed out of heaven.

All the names of Daniel 10 pull back the spiritual curtain and gives us a brief glimpse into a world of spiritual warfare that is very real, though it rages unseen to the physical eye. There's God, Jesus, King Cyrus, Daniel, the Angel Gabriel, the Archangel Michael, and all the believers in our Lord and Savior Jesus Christ, and God Almighty and all the angels in heaven. We are in a spiritual warfare with Satan, the fallen angels, and demons, in Daniel chapter 10. In the third year of Cyrus the Persian Conqueror of Babylon. Daniel sees a vision of a man, but clearly a supernatural being, who tells him that he is currently engaged in battle with the prince of Persia, in which he is assisted by Michael, your prince. the angel Gabriel, must soon return to the combat.

In Matthew 25:41, this is Jesus Christ speaking, then he will also say to those on the left hand, Depart from me, you accursed, into the eternal fire prepared for the devil and his angels.

In Matthew 25:31, 33, When the Son of Man comes in his glory, and all the angels with him, he will sit upon his glorious throne, and all the nations will be assembled before him, And he will separate them one from another, as a shepherd separates the sheeps from the goats. He will place the sheep on his right and the goats on his left.

What does it mean to separate the sheep from the goats?

This term refers to Jesus's prophecy in the New Testament (Matthew 25:32), that the sheep (that is, the compassionate) will sit on God's right hand (and find salvation), and the goats (the hard-hearted) will sit on the left (and be sent to damnation).

So, what does God say about protecting his children?

Parents and children need God's protection. God is our deliverer from trouble and enemies, and we should protect kids from people who seek their harm as an extension of our love for him.

As a father, I had to learn to protect my family, my two sons, and my grandchild.

The first thing I did was quit drinking alcohol and doing drugs. Although I was a believer of God Almighty, Jesus Christ our Savior, and went to church, I was still drinking and doing drugs. I was going to need help. In Revelations 3:14, 17 talks about being lukewarm, it reads: To the angel of the church in Laodicea, write this: The Amen, the faithful and true witness, the source of God's creation, says this: "I will know your works; I know that you are neither cold nor hot. I wish you were either cold or hot. So, because you are lukewarm, neither hot nor cold, I will spit you out of my mouth. For you say, 'I am rich and affluent and have no need for anything, and yet do you not realize that you are wretched, pitiable, poor, blind, and naked."

So, I, John Michael Gurule, did not want to be a miserable person.

So, what I did is I gave my life to the Lord one hundred percent. I put myself into the hospital for 90 days, I got off all my medications, and cleaned myself up. I went to the bible and I found the scriptures in Romans 10:8, 10. It reads: But what does it say? "The word is near you, in your mouth and in your heart." (that is, the word of faith that we preach). For, if you confess with your mouth that Jesus is Lord and believe in your heart that God raised him from the dead, you will be saved. For one believes with the heart and so is justified, and one confesses with the mouth and so is saved.

Then I went to a Catholic Christian store to buy a St. Michael The Archangel Card. This is the second half of my story, in my second book. The next thing I'm doing is relearning the Ten Commandments. In order to be a responsible parent and a person worth listening to, is to hear God's Word, be obedient and to act accordingly. Biblical obedience to God means to hear, trust, submit and surrender to God and His Word. The objective is a goal, to better myself and to learn obedience, and teach our children the meaning of obedience to God's Word. In the book of Deuteronomy 6: 4-10, tells you to teach your children the Ten Commandments, and it reads: Hear O Israel! The Lord is our God, the Lord alone! Therefore, you shall love the Lord, your God, with your whole heart, and with your whole being, and with your whole strength. Take to heart these words which I command you today. Keep repeating them to your children. Recite them when you are at home and when you are away, when you lie down and when you get up. Bind them on your arms as a sign and let them be as a pendant on your forehead. Write them on the doorposts of your houses and on your gates. When the Lord your God, brings you into the land which he swore to your ancestors, to Abraham, Isaac and Jacob, that he would give you, a land with find, large cities that you did not build.

These are the Ten Commandments; Deuteronomy 5:6, 21:

I am the Lord your God who brought you out of the land of Egypt, out of the house of slavery.

Number One: You shall not have other gods beside me. You shall not make for yourself an idol or a likeness of anything in the heavens above or on the earth below or in the waters beneath the earth. You shall not bow down before them or serve them. For I, the Lord, your God, am a jealous God, bringing punishment for their parents' wickedness on the children of those who hate me, down to the third and fourth generation, but showing love down to the thousandth generation of those who love me and keep my commandments.

Number Two: You shall not invoke the name of the Lord, your God, in vain. For the Lord will not leave unpunished anyone who invokes his name in vain.

Number Three: Observe the sabbath day—keep it holy, as the Lord, your God, commanded you. Six days you may labor and do all your work, but the seventh day is a sabbath of the Lord your God. You shall not do any work, either you, your son or your daughter, your male or female slave, your ox or donkey or any work animal, or the resident alien within your gates, so that your male and female slave may rest as you do. Remember that you too were once slaves in the land of Egypt, and the Lord, your God, brought you out from there with a strong hand and out-stretched arm. That is why the Lord, your God, has commanded you to observe the sabbath day.

Number Four: Honor your father and your mother, as the Lord, your God, has commanded you, that you may have a long life and that you may prosper in the land the Lord your God is giving you.

Number Five: You shall not kill.

Number Six: You shall not commit adultery.

Number Seven: You shall not steal.

Number Eight: You shall not bear dishonest witness against your neighbor.

Number Nine: You shall not cover your neighbor's wife.

Number Ten: You shall not desire your neighbor's house or field, his male or female slave, his ox or donkey, or anything that belongs to your neighbor.

According to the biblical narrative, the first set of tablets, inscribed by the finger of God, Exodus 31:18, were smashed by Moses when he was enraged by the sight of the children of Israel worshipping a golden calf Exodus 32:19 and the second tablet was later chiseled out by Moses and rewritten by God, Exodus 34:1.

Jesus Two-Commandment scripture, Matthew 22:37-40.

Jesus said to them, "You shall love the Lord, your God, with all your heart, with all your soul, and with all your mind. This is the greatest and the first commandment. The second is like it: You shall love your neighbor as yourself. The whole law and the prophets depend on these two commandments."

Why follow the commandments of God Almighty and Jesus our Savior?

God gave us the Ten Commandments. Deuteronomy 5:6, 21 and Jesus gave us the two commandments, Matthew 22: 37-40.

And the reason is, that both God and Jesus love us and wants us to live good lives - lives that are peaceful, happy and productive. God isn't a harsh, angry judge just waiting for us to get out of line so he can punish us. He is our loving, heavenly Father, who knows what is best for us.

Don't forget we have an enemy Satan, fallen angels and demons.

In John Chapter 20, the disciples shouted that they had seen Jesus raised from the grave, but Thomas' doubt kept him from believing in the miracle of salvation. John 20: Then he said to Thomas, "Put your finger here and see my hands, and bring your hand and put it into my side, and do not be unbelieving, but believe.

1 Peter 5: 6, 8, So humble yourselves under the mighty hand of God, that he may exalt you in due time. Cast all your worries upon him because he cares for you. Be sober and vigilant. Your opponent the devil is prowling around like a roaring lion looking for someone to devour.

It is important for family, parents, children and all Christian relationships to obey the commandments of God; children obey your parents in the Lord, trusting in the Lord. We need to learn to Fight Spiritual Battles.

Ephesians 6: 1, 20, Children, obey your parents in the Lord, for this is right. Honor your father and mother. This is the first commandment with a promise, that it may go well with you and that you may have a long life on earth. Fathers: do not provoke your children to anger but bring them up with the training and instruction of the Lord.

Slaves, be obedient to your human masters with fear and trembling, in sincerity of heart, as to Christ, not only when being watched, as currying favor, but as slaves of Christ, doing the will of God from the heart, willingly serving the Lord and not human beings, knowing that each will be requited from the Lord for whatever good he does, whether he is slave or free. Masters, act in the same way toward them, and stop bullying, knowing that both they and you have a Master in heaven and that with him there is no partiality.

Finally, draw your strength from the Lord and from his mighty power. Put on the armor of God so that you may be able to stand firm against the tactics of the devil. For our struggle is not with flesh and blood but with the principalities, with the powers, with the world rules of this present darkness, with the evil spirits in the heavens.

Therefore, put on the armor of God, that you may be able to resist on the evil day and, having done everything, to hold your ground. So, stand fast with your loins girded in truth, clothed with righteousness as a breastplate, and your feet shod in readiness for the gospel of peace. In all circumstances, hold fait as a shield, to quench all the flaming arrows of the evil one. And take the helmet of salvation and the sword of the Spirit, which is the word of God. With all prayer and supplication, pray at every opportunity in the Spirit. To that end, be watchful with all perseverance and supplication for all the holy ones and also for me, that speech may be given me to open my mouth, to make known with boldness the mystery of the gospel for which I am an ambassador in chains, so that I may have the courage to speak as I must.

St Paul viewed himself not merely as a lowly prisoner, but as "an ambassador in chains". He was a representative of the King of Kings, and the Lord of Lords, Jesus Christ.

Further, Paul noted that declaring God's truth boldly was the right thing to do. He did not view being quiet about his faith as honorable. Instead, he asked for faith to speak even more boldly about Christ. This was quite admirable given the fact that he was already imprisoned because of his preaching of the gospel. Paul refused to back down, and rather wanted to become even bolder in presenting the good news of Jesus Christ.

St. Peter and St. Paul, Apostles, Martyrs. June 29 is the Feast day of St. Peter and St. Paul. This feast day commemorates the martyrdom of the two great Apostles, assigned by tradition to the same day of June in the year 67 AD-64 AD. They had been imprisoned in the famous Mamertine Prison of Rome and both had foreseen their approaching death. Saint Peter was crucified upside down; Saint Paul, a Roman citizen, was slain and beheaded by the sword.

St. Peter and St. Paul are said to have been incarcerated in the jail by the Emperor Nero. Peter was then crucified, upside down, in AD 64. He was buried on a low hill on which, 250 years, later, the Emperor Constantine built the first Basilica of St. Peter.

The Persecution under Nero in which Paul and Peter were Honored at Rome with Martyrdom in Behalf of Religion.

When the government of Emperor Nero was now firmly established, he began to plunge into unholy pursuits, and armed himself even against the religion of the God of the universe.

Paul was beheaded, according to tradition, on the Ostian way, at the spot now occupied by the Abbey of the Three Fountains, which are said to have sprung up at the spots where Paul's head struck the ground three times after the decapitation are still shown, as also the pillar to which he is supposed to have been bound! In the fourth century, at the same time that Peter's remains were transferred to the Vatican, Paul's remains are said to have been buried in the Basilica of St. Paul, which occupied the site now marked by the church of San Paolo Fuori Le Mura. There is nothing improbable in the traditions as to the spot where Paul and Peter met their death.

Is there a risk to following and serving our Lord and Savior Jesus Christ?

There are three signs where God is telling you to take a risk to reap a reward.

1) 2 Corinthians 9: 6, 9, Consider this: whoever sows sparingly will also reap sparingly, and whoever sows bountifully will also reap bountifully. Each must do as already determined, without sadness or compulsion, for God loves a cheerful giver. Moreover, God is able to make every grace abundant for you, so that in all things, always having all you need, you may have an abundance for every good work. As it is written: "He scatters abroad, he gives to the poor; his righteousness endures forever."

2) Proverbs 4:20, 27,

My son, to my words be attentive,
    to my sayings incline your ear;
Let them not slip from your sight,
    keep them within your heart;
For they are life to those who find them,
    bringing health to one's whole being.
With all vigilance guard your heart,
    for in it are the sources of life.
Dishonest mouth put away from you,
    deceitful lips put far from you.
Let your eyes look straight ahead
    and your gaze be focused forward.
Survey the path for your feet,
    and all your ways will be sure.
Turn neither to right nor to left,
    keep your foot far from evil.

Proverbs 4:23, warns us to guard our hearts, so we need to be careful that we are not living recklessly and exposing ourselves to unnecessary emotional or physical dangers.

In Luke 14:25-33, Jesus teaches us that we must count the cost of following him. I love how honest Jesus is with us. Yes, following Jesus will bring us the most joy and greatest rewards for eternity. Yes, grace is free. But following God will still be risky and costly.

Does Jesus pray for us?

In the gospel of John 17:15, 26, Jesus says, "I do not ask that you take them out of the world but that you keep them from the evil one. They do not belong to the world any more than I belong to the world. Consecrate them in the truth. Your word is truth. As you sent me into the world, so I sent them into the world. And I consecrate myself for them, so that they also may be consecrated in truth.

I pray not only for them, but also for those who will believe in me through their word, so that they may all be one, as you, Father, are in me and I in you, that they also may be in us, that the world may believe that you sent me. And I have given them the glory you gave me, so that they may be one, as we are one; I in them and you in me, that they may be brought to perfection as one, that the world may know that you sent me, and that you loved them even as you loved me. Father, they are your gift to me. I wish that where I am they also may be with me, that they may see my glory that you gave me, because you loved me before the foundation of the world. Righteous Father, the world also does not know you, but I know you, and they know that you sent me. I made known to them your name and I will make it known, that the love with which you loved me may be in them and I in them.

Jesus teaches us to pray, in Luke 11:1, 4

He was praying in a certain place, and when he had finished, one of his disciples said to him, "teach us to pray just as John taught his disciples." He said to them, "When you pray, say:

Father, hallowed be your name,
    your kingdom come.
    give us each day our daily bread
    and forgive us our sins
    for we ourselves forgive everyone in
        debt to us,
    and do not subject us to the final test.

Why should we pray again?

This is a Red Alert, Rev 12:17, says the dragon became angry with the woman and went off to wage war against the rest of her offspring, those who keep God's commandments and bear witness to Jesus. It took its position on the sand of the sea. The woman, Israel, church.

This is a Red Alert!

Revelation 12:7, 9, says that then war broke out in heaven; Michael and his angels battled against the dragon. The dragon and its angels fought back, but they did not prevail and there was no longer any place for them in heaven. The huge dragon, the ancient serpent, who is called the Devil and Satan, who deceived the whole world, was thrown down to earth, and its angels were thrown down with it.

This is the Red Alert!

Revelation 12:12,14, Therefore, rejoice, you heavens, and you who dwell in them. But woe to you, earth and sea, for the Devil has come down to you in great fury, for he knows he has but a short time.

When the dragon saw that it had been thrown down to the earth, it pursued the woman who had given birth to the male child. But the woman was given the two wings of the great eagle, so that she could fly to her place in the desert, where, far from the serpent, she was taken care of for a year, two years, and a half-year.

So, what I did here was to give everyone a heads up on who are the keys players in Daniel chapter ten, from the earth to the second heaven to the third heaven. Ephesians 6:11, 12 tells us we can overcome by putting on the whole armor of God, that you may be able to stand against the wiles of the devil. For we do not wrestle against flesh and blood, but against principalities, against powers, against the rulers of the darkness of this age, against spiritual hosts of wickedness in the heavenly places.

Ephesians 6:18, 19, With all prayer and supplication, pray at every opportunity in the Spirit. To that end, be watchful with all perseverance and supplication for all the holy ones and also for me, that speech may be given me to open my mouth, to make known with boldness the mystery of the gospel for which I am an ambassador in chains, so that I may have the courage to speak as I must.

Now we go back to the story in the St Michael Card. It is he who prepares for their return from the Persian captivity, from chapter five.

Jeremiah 29: 10, 13, reads: For thus says the Lord: Only after seventy years have elapsed for Babylon will I deal with you and fulfill for you my promise to bring you back to this place. For I know well the plans I have in mind for you—oracle of the Lord—plans for your welfare and not for woe, so as to give you a future of hope. When you call to me, and come and pray to me, I will listen to you. When you look for me, you will find me. Yes, when you seek me with all your heart.

Ezra 1:1, 6, Ezra relates the story of two returns from Babylon - the first led by Zerubbabel to rebuild the temple, and the second under the leadership of Ezra to rebuild the spiritual condition of the people.

The call of Jeremiah 1: 4, 10, The word of the Lord came to me: Before I formed you in the womb I knew you, before you were born I dedicated you, a prophet to the nations I appointed you. "Ah, Lord God, I said, I do not know how to speak. I am too young." But the Lord answered me, Do not say, "I am too young." To whomever I send you, you shall go; whatever I command you, you shall speak. Do not be afraid of the, for I am with you to deliver you—oracle of the Lord. Then the Lord extended his hand and touched my mouth, saying to me: See, I place my words in your mouth! Today I appoint you over nations and over kingdoms, to uproot and to tear down, to destroy and to demolish, to build and to plant.

Jeremiah was destined to become a prophet before his birth; I knew you, I loved you and I chose you.

Autobiography on page 79 of my first book, A Forty Year Journey with God in Albuquerque New Mexico reads; My name is John Michael Gurule. I'm fifty-five years old. As of February 28, 2013, I'm a Jesus Christ believer.

Right before I was born, I had a vision. Notice that I said before I was born, I have seen myself playing ball in heaven with someone I could not see. I looked like a boy filled with the Holy Spirit, it was Me. "I am your Creator. You were in my care even before you were born." Isaiah 44:2.

The Spirit of the Lord moves in the return of the Jewish people back to Jerusalem and the rebuilding of the Second Temple.

Jerusalem the Holy City

For Christians, Jerusalem is also the place where Jesus preached, died and was resurrected. Many also see the city as central to the second coming of Jesus. Jerusalem is now a major pilgrimage site for Christians from around the world. That's why this Holy City Jerusalem is very important.

In Jeremiah 29:14, in the rebuilding of the second temple.

I will let you find me—oracle of the Lord—and I will change your lot; I will gather you together from all the nations and all the places to which I have banished you—oracle of the Lord—and bring you back to the place from which I have exiled you.

Cyrus the Great as foretold in Bible Prophecy

Isaiah 44:24, 28, Cyrus, Anointed of the Lord, Agent of Israel's Liberation.

Thus says the Lord, your redeemer, who formed you from the womb: I am the Lord, who made all things, who alone stretched out the heavens, I spread out the earth by myself. I bring to nought the omens of babblers, make fools of diviners; turn back the wise and make their knowledge foolish. I confirm the words of my servant, carry out the plan my messengers announce. I say to Jerusalem, Be inhabited! To the cities of Judah, Be rebuilt! I will raise up their ruins. I say to the deep, Be dry! I will dry up your rivers. I say of Cyrus, My shepherd! He carries out my every wish, saying of Jerusalem, "Let it be rebuilt," and of the temple, "Lay its foundations."

Isaiah 45:1,3, Thus says the Lord to his anointed, Cyrus, whose right hand I grasp, subduing nations before him, stripping kings of their strength, opening doors before him, leaving the gates unbarred; I will go before you and level the mountains; bronze doors I will shatter, iron bars I will snap. I will give you treasures of darkness, riches hidden away, that you may know I am the Lord, the God of Israel, who calls you by name.

The Fall of Babylon, Isaiah 47:1, 4:

Come down, sit in the dust, virgin daughter Babylon; sit on the ground, dethroned, daughter of the Chaldeans. No longer shall you be called dainty and delicate. Take the millstone and grind floor, remove your veil; strip off your skirt, bare your legs, cross through the streams. Your nakedness shall be uncovered, and your shame be seen; I will take vengeance, I will yield to no entreaty, says our redeemer, whose name is the Lord of Hosts, the Holy One of Israel.

Isaiah chapters 44-45, which were written about 700 B.C., call King Cyrus by name over 100 years before his birth and describe his reign in detail.

The Jewish text confirms Cyrus own information that he was chosen by the Supreme God Almighty to liberate the Jewish people from Babylon.

In the book of Ezra 1:1, 11, In the first year of Cyrus, King of Persia, in order to fulfill the word of the Lord spoken by Jeremiah, the Lord stirred up the spirit of Cyrus king of Persia to issue a proclamation throughout his entire kingdom, both by word of mouth and in writing: Thus says Cyrus, king of Persia: All kingdoms of the earth the Lord, the God of heaven, has given to me, and he has charged me to build him a house in Jerusalem, which is in Judah. Those among you who belong to any part of his people, may their God be with them! Let them go up to Jerusalem in Judah to build the house of the Lord the God of Israel, that is, the God who is in Jerusalem. Let all those who have survived, in whatever place they may have lived, be assisted by the people of that place with silver, gold, goods, and livestock, together with voluntary offerings for the house of God in Jerusalem.

Then the heads of ancestral houses of Judah and Benjamin and the priests and Levites—everyone, that is, whose spirit had been stirred up by God—prepared to go up to build the house of the Lord in Jerusalem. All their neighbors gave them help in every way, with silver, gold, goods, livestock, and many precious gifts, besides all their voluntary offerings. King Cyrus, too, had the vessels of the house of the Lord brought forth that Nebuchadnezzar had taken from Jerusalem and placed in the house of his god. Cyrus, king of Persia, had them brought forth by the treasurer Mithredath, who counted them out to Sheshbazzar, prince of Judah. This was the inventory: baskets of goldware, thirty; baskets of silverware, one thousand and twenty nine; golden bowls, thirty; silver bowls, four hundred and ten; other vessels, one thousand. Total of the gold and silver vessels: five thousand four hundred. All these Sheshbazzar took with him when the exiles were brought up from Babylon to Jerusalem.

Cyrus in Babylon and the Jewish connection.

Cyrus the Great is unconditionally praised in the Jewish sources. It is likely that, after the Persian conquest of Babylon, Cyrus had commenced his relationship with the Jewish leaders in exile, and that he later was considered as anointed by God.

The Hebrew Bible states that Cyrus issued the decree of liberation to the Jews. Cyrus' edict for the rebuilding of the Temple in Jerusalem marked a great epoch in the history of the Jewish people. According to Ezra 4:1,6, when the enemies of Judah and Benjamin heard that the exiles were building a temple for the Lord, the God of Israel, they approached Zerubbabel and the heads of ancestral houses and said to them, "Let us build with you, for we see your God just as you do, and we have sacrificed to him since the days of Esarhaddon, king of Assyria, who brought us here. But Zerubbabel, Jeshua, and the rest of the heads of ancestral houses of Israel answered them, "It is not your responsibility to build with us a house for our God, but we alone must build it for the Lord, the God of Israel, as Cyrus, king of Persia, has commanded us." Thereupon the local inhabitants discouraged the people of Judah and frightened them off from building. They also bribed counselors to work against them and to frustrate their plans during all the years of Cyrus, king of Persia, and even into the reign of Darius, king of Persia.

In the reign of Ahasuerus, at the beginning of his reign, they prepared a written accusation against the inhabitants of Judah and Jerusalem.

Who were the enemies against rebuilding the temple?

Ezra 4:1, 3, When the enemies of Judah and Benjamin heard that the exiles were building a temple for the Lord, the God of Israel, they approached Zerubbabel and the heads of ancestral houses and said to them, "Let us build with you, for we see your God just as you do, and we have sacrificed to him since the days of Esarhaddon, king of Assyria, who brought us here. But Zerubbabel, Jeshua, and the rest of the heads of ancestral houses of Israel answered them, "It is not your responsibility to build with us a house for our God, but we alone must build it for the Lord, the God of Israel, as Cyrus, king of Persia, has commanded us."

Who are the enemies, adversaries of God?

A person, group, or force that opposes or attacks; opponent; enemy; foe. A person, group, etc., that is an opponent in a contest; contestant. The Adversary, the devil; Satan.

Who was the King Esarhaddon, (reigned 681-669 B.C.E.) was the third king of the Sargonid Dynasty of the Neo-Assyrian Empire. He was the youngest son of King Sennacherib. (reign 705-681 B.C.E.)

In 1 Chronicles 21:15, the same "Angel of the Lord" is seen by David to stand "between the earth and the heaven, with a drawn sword in his hand stretch out against Jerusalem. Later, in II Kings 19:35, the angel kills 185,000 men of Sennacherib's Assyrian army, thereby saving Hezekian's Jerusalem.

In the book of II Kings 19:37 states: when he was worshiping in the temple of his god Nisroch, his sons Adrammelech and Sharezer struck him down with the sword and fled into the land of Ararat. His son Esarhaddon resigned in his place.

After the Elamites killed his eldest son and crown prince, Ashur-nadin-shumi, Sennacherib originally designated his second eldest son, Arda-Mulissu, as his heir. Her later replaced him with a younger son, Esarhaddon, in 684 B.C. for unknown reasons. Sennacherib ignored Arda-Mulissu's repeated appeals to be reinstated as heir. In 681 B.C., Arda-Mulissu and another son assaulted and murdered Sennacherib, hoping to seize power for themselves. Esarhaddon raised an army and seized Nineveh, installing himself as king as intended by Sennacherib.

Esarhaddon, his son, became king; another ancient Babylonian letter, although somewhat damaged, contains the following sentence: Thy son Arda-Mulissi is going to kill thee. Arda-Mulissi, the Adrammelech of II Kings 19:37, was the son of Sennacherib, who did end up assassinating him. Evidently, he teamed up with his brother Nabu-sarru-usur (biblical Sharezer) to kill their father - which they did while he was worshiping in a temple. Esarhaddon returned to take control of Assyria.

In Ezra 4:1, 3 reads: when the enemies of Judah and Benjamin heard that the exiles were building a temple for the Lord, the God of Israel, they approached Zerubbabel and the heads of ancestral houses and said to them, "Let us build with you, for we see your God just as you do, and we have sacrificed to him since the days of Esarhaddon, king of Assyria, who brought us here. But Zerubbabel, Jeshua, and the rest of the heads of ancestral houses of Israel answered them, "It is not your responsibility to build with us a house for our God, but we alone must build it for the Lord, the God of Israel, as Cyrus, king of Persia, has commanded us."

Ezra 4:4, 8. Thereupon the local inhabitants discouraged the people of Judah and frightened them off from building. They also bribed counselors to work against them and to frustrate their plans during all the years of Cyrus, king of Persia, and even into the reign of Darius, king of Persia. In the reign of Ahasuerus, at the beginning of his reign, they prepared a written accusation against the inhabitants of Judah and Jerusalem. Again, in the time of Artaxerxes, Tabeel and the rest of his fellow officials, in concert with Mithredath, wrote to Artaxerxes, king of Persia. The document was written in Aramaic and was accompanied by a translation.

In the days of Artaxerxes also, Ezra 4:8, 10. Then, Rehum, the governor, and Shimshai, the scribe, wrote the following letter against Jerusalem to King Artaxerxes: Rehum, the governor, Shimshai, the scribe, and their fellow officials, judges, legates, and agents from among the Persians,

Urukians, Babylonians, Susians (that is, Elamites), and the other peoples whom the great and illustrious Osnappar transported and settled in the city of Samaria and elsewhere in the province West-of-Euphrates, as follows:

Samaritans attempts to stop the work, the rebuilding of the 2nd temple. These are the people complaining ...

From Rehum the commander, Shimshai the scribe and the rest of their companions, representatives of the Dinaites, the Apharsathchites, the Tarpelites, the people of Persia and Erech and Babylon and Shushan, the Dehavites, the Elamites, and the rest of the nations whom the great and noble Osnapper took captive and settled in the cities of Samaria and the remainder beyond the River, and so forth.

This is the copy of the letter that they sent him.

Ezra 4, 11,12, To King Artaxerxes, your servants, the men of West-of-Euphrates, as follows: Let it be known to the king that the Jews who came up from you to us have arrived at Jerusalem and are now rebuilding this rebellious and evil city. They are completing its walls, and the foundations have already been laid.

Ezra 4:12 to 1, Complains of the rebuilding of 2nd temple.

Ezra 4:17 to 22, Artaxerxes responds to Rehum the Commander, to Shimshai the Scribe, to the rest of their companions who dwell in Samaria, and to the remainder, Beyond the River.

Now I'm going to go to verses Ezra 4, 21,22. Give orders, therefore, to stop these men. This city may not be rebuilt until a further decree has been issued by me. Take care that you do not neglect this matter. Why should evil increase to harm the throne?

Ezra 4:2, they approached Zerubbabel and the heads of ancestral houses and said to them, Let us build with you, for we seek your God just as you do, and we have sacrificed to him since the days of Esarhaddon, king of Assyria, who brought us here.

Esarhaddon, king of Assyria, is the son of King Sennacherib of Assyria.

2 Chronicles 32:1, 3, But after all this and all Hezekiah's fidelity, there came Sennacherib, king of Assyria. He invaded Judah and besieged the fortified cities, intending to breach and take them. When Hezekiah saw that Sennacherib was coming with the intention of attacking Jerusalem, he took the advice of his princes and warriors to stop the waters of the springs outside the city; they promised their help.

So it was King Esarhaddon who brought these people to the cities of Samaria. Esarhaddon king of Assyria: the ememies represent themselves as descendants of foreigners forcibly resettled in the Samaria region after the incorporation of Northern Kingdom into the Assyrian empire; (722 B.C.; 2 Kings 17:24) we have no record of a settlement under Esarhaddon (681-669 B.C.); the Aramaic source (Ezra 4:10) refers to a different resettlement under Osnappar, Ashurbanipal (668-627 B.C.)

The offer of a dangerous alliance. Adversaries try to join the work of building of the temple of God. Now when the adversaries: Judea was not completely empty of inhabitants in two generations of captivity. There was a remnant descended from the lowest and poorest of the land that was left behind in the exile, combined with the few who had drifted into the largely desolate area. These people were not happy that Judah and Benjamin had come back to Judea and thus they were their adversaries.

These were the early Samaritans, those who were brought into the lands of the former Kingdom of Israel after its fall to the Assyrians, who intermarried with those left behind from the exile. In the two generations of exile after the fall of the Kingdom of Judah, they had also expanded somewhat into the lands of Judah.

The Samaritans continued as a people into New Testament times. Because the Samaritans had some historical connection to the people of Israel, their faith was a combination of law and ritual from the Law of Moses and various superstitions. Most Jews in Jesus time despised the Samaritans, even more than Gentiles, because they were, religiously speaking, half-breeds who had an eclectic mongrel faith. This context is essential in understanding the Parable of the Good Samaritan in Luke 10:25, 37.

2 Kings 17:24, tells the attitude of the Samaritans: They feared the Lord yet served their own gods; according to the rituals of the nations from among whom they were away.

In John 4:1, 42, Jesus talks to a Samaritan woman.

Now when Jesus learned that the Pharisees had heard that Jesus was making and baptizing more disciples than John (although Jesus himself not was not baptizing, just his disciples), he left Judea and returned to Galilee.

He had to pass through Samaria. So he came to a town of Samaria called Sychar, near the plot of land that Jacob had given to his son Joseph. Jacob's well was there. Jesus, tired from his journey, sat down there at the well. It was about noon.

A woman of Samaria came to draw water. Jesus said to her, "Give me a drink." His disciples had gone into the town to buy food. The Samaritan woman said to him, "How can you, a Jew, ask me, a Samaritan woman, for a drink?" (For Jews use nothing in common with Samaritans.) Jesus answered and said to her, "If you knew the gift of God and who is saying to you, 'Give me a drink', you would have asked him and he would have given you living water. The woman said to him, "Sir, you do not even have a bucket and the well is deep; where then can you get this living water? Are you greater than our father Jacob, who gave us this well and drank from it himself with his children and his flocks?" Jesus answered and said to her, "Everyone who drinks this water will be thirsty again; but whoever drinks the water I shall give will never thirst; the water I shall give will become in him a spring of water welling up to eternal life. The woman said to him, "Sir, give me this water, so that I may not be thirsty or have to keep coming here to draw water."

Jesus said to her, "Go call your husband and come back." The woman answered and said to him, "I do not have a husband." Jesus answered her, "You are right in saying, 'I do not have a husband. For you have had five husbands, and the one you have now is not your husband. What you have said is true." The woman said to him, "Sir, I can see that you are a prophet. Our ancestors worshiped on this mountain; but your people say that the place to worship is in Jerusalem. Jesus said to her, "Believe me, woman, the hour is coming when you will worship the Father neither on the mountain nor in Jerusalem. You people worship what you do not understand; we worship what we understand, because salvation is from the Jews. But the hour is coming, and is now here, when true worshipers will worship the Father in Spirit and truth; and indeed, the Father seeks such people to worship him. God is Spirit, and those who worship him must worship in Spirit and truth." The woman said to him, "I know that the Messiah is coming, the one called the Anointed; when he comes, he will tell us everything." Jesus sad to her, "I am he, the one who is speaking to you."

At that moment his disciples returned, and were amazed that he was talking with a woman, but still no one said, "What are you looking for?" or "Why are you talking to her?" The woman left her water jar and went into the town and said to the people, "Come see a man who told me everything I have done. Could he possibly be the Messiah?" They went out of the town and came to him. Meanwhile, the disciples urged him, "Rabbi, eat." But he said to them "I have food to eat of which you do not know." So the disciples said to one another, "Could someone have brought him something to eat?" Jesus said to them, "My food is to do the will of the one who sent me and to finish his work. Do you not say, 'In four months the harvest will be here'? I tell you, look up and see the fields ripe for the harvest. The reaper is already receiving his payment and gathering crops for eternal life, so that the sower and reaper can rejoice together. For here the saying is verified that 'One sows, and another reaps. I sent you to reap what you have not worked for; others have done the work, and you are sharing the fruits of their work."

Many of the Samaritans of that town began to believe in him because of the word of the woman who testified, "He told me everything I have done." When the Samaritans came to him, they invited him to stay with them; and he stayed there two days. Many more began to believe in him because of his word, and they said to the woman, "We no longer believe because of your word; for we have heard for ourselves, and we know that this is truly the savior of the world."

The Fields Are Ripe For Harvest.

Do you not say, 'There are yet four months, and then comes the harvest? Behold, I say to you, lift up your eyes and look on the fields, that they are ripe for harvest.' (John 4:35)

Jesus said these words to His disciples as they were in Samaria. He had just spoken to a Samaritan woman at the well outside the city. She returned and told the men of the city about Jesus and they were now coming out to see Him. He said the fields were ripe for harvest, meaning there was success to be had in preaching the gospel in that place.

As we are still working to preach the gospel today, let us consider Jesus' statement and the circumstances surrounding it.

What did Jesus see that caused him to say that the fields were ripe for harvest? First, he saw people who were lost. Jesus desired that the lost would be saved (Matthew 23:37; Luke 15:1, 7). His mission in coming to earth was to seek and to save that which was lost (Luke 19:10). Here he found a woman who was living in adultery and caught up in false religion (John 4:17, 18, 20). The false religion was found among her fellow countrymen as well. These people were lost in sin. They needed a Savior.

Jesus also saw people who were interested. This is very important. After Jesus struck up the conversation with the Samaritan woman, she expressed her interest by asking Jesus for the water He said he could provide (John 4:15) and by questioning Him about proper worship practices (John 4:19, 20). The people of the city came out to the well to hear Jesus because they were interested in what He had to say (John 4:30). It was at this point when Jesus made this statement: The fields are ripe for harvest (John 4:35).

What Did the People Need?

The fields were ripe for harvest in Samaria. But just like crops in the fields cannot harvest themselves, someone else had to labor for the harvest to happen. So, the first thing they needed was a willing teacher. Historically, the Jews and Samaritans did not have friendly relations with one another. The woman Jesus met at the well was surprised that He even spoke to her:

How is it that you, being a Jew, ask me for a drink since I am a Samaritan woman? John added the parenthetical statement to explain this: For Jews have no dealing with Samaritans (John 4:9). Jesus was willing to teach people, regardless of their background. This should not be surprising since He also died for all people, regardless of their background (John 3:16; Ephesians 2:13, 16).

It was important that these people had someone willing to teach them, but this would not do any good without the proper message from the teacher. Jesus had a different message from all others. The message from the Samaritans was that they were to worship on the mountain; neither in this mountain nor in Jerusalem. (John 4:21). She needed His message. He was the one with the "words of eternal life" (John 6:88). Jesus taught the gospel. That is what this woman, and everyone else - needed.

Are the Fields Ripe for Harvest Today?

If Jesus were here today, would He be telling us to look on the fields, that they are ripe for harvest? It is certainly true that people are lost now just as they were then. This will be true as long as the earth stands. Paul wrote, For all have sinned, and fall short of the glory of God (Romans 3:23). This condition still exist today.

Are people interested in Christ? That is another matter and it may depend on where you are. In some places, there may be a great interest in spiritual things but that will not be the case everywhere. Some people simply do not want to hear the truth. We can't force people to accept Christ. So, when we encounter people who are not interested, we should move on. In these instances, the disciples were told to shake the dust off your feet (Matthew 10:14; Acts 13:50, 51)

However, it is important to note that the disciples shook the dust off their feet and moved on after the gospel had been preached. They did not decide that the people would probably not be receptive and so they should just move on without teaching them. Instead, they gave the people the chance to hear the gospel and reject it for themselves. We cannot always know people's hearts so we must plant the seed wherever possible. Give them the chance to reject the message, and do not reject it for them. In giving them the chance to reject the message, we are also giving them the chance to accept it which leads to salvation. So, we should understand that it is likely for most people to be uninterested in the gospel but that does not mean we should give up in efforts to reach the lost.

What Do People Need Today?

Just as the people of Samaria needed a willing teacher, people today need willing teachers as well. After telling the Romans that whoever will call on the name of the Lord will be saved (Romans 10:13), Paul went on to discuss the importance of those who preach the gospel: How then will they call on Him in whom they have not believed? How will they believe in Him whom they have not heard? And how will they hear without a preacher? How will they preach unless they are sent? Just as it is written, How beautiful are the feet of those who bring good news of good things (Romans 10:14, 15). The lost need to be taught. It is important to have men who have dedicated their lives to this work to do it.

However, it is not the responsibility of the preacher to teach others.

All Christians much be ready to teach when opportunities arise (1 Peter 3:15). Furthermore, just as God shows no partiality (Acts 10:34, 35), we must not either (James 2:1, 9). We should be willing to teach others regardless of their race, gender, class, background, or any other factor.

Not only is it important to have willing teachers, but they must have the right message. Like Jesus did, we must simply preach the gospel. This is the message that people need to hear (Romans 1:16). We change or add to the message based upon the whims of the people, nor do we do them any favors by doing this. We are obligated to please God first. Paul said, "Am I now currying favor with human beings or God? Or am I seeking to please people? If I were seeking to please people, I would not be a slave of Christ." (Galatians 1:10)

Instead of relying upon the schemes that many use to try and bring others to Christ, we must simply use the method that Jesus and the apostles used, preaching the gospel. Instead of changing the message, adding to it, or taking parts out of it, we should trust in God and the word that He revealed. The gospel, in its entirety and simplicity, is still today, the power of God for salvation. (Romans 1:16)

So, these people coming out of Samaria wrote a letter to Artaxerxes, wanting to stop the building of Jerusalem.

This Rehum the commander, Shimshai the scribe, and the rest of their companions, and the rest of the nations whom the great and noble Osnapper took captive and settled in the cities of Samaria and the remainder beyond the River, and so forth.

Artaxerxes gave orders, therefore, to stop these men. This city Jerusalem may not be rebuilt until a further decree has been issued by me. (Ezra 4:18, 22)

Ezra 4:23, 24, As soon as a copy of King Artaxerxes' letter had been read before Rehum, the governor, Shimshai, the scribe, and their fellow officials, they immediately went to the Jews in Jerusalem and stopped their work by force of arms. As a result, work on the house of God in Jerusalem ceased. This interruption lasted until the second year of the reign of Darius, king of Persia.

Ezra 4, Samaritan attempts to stop the work of second building of the temple of God.

2 Kings 17:24, tells the attitude of the Samaritans: They feared the Lord yet served their own gods; according to the rituals of the nations from among whom they were carried away, referring to Jews.

Ezra 4:23, 24, the worked ceased for 16 long years.

Ezra 5, Then the prophet Haggai and Zechariah, the son of Iddo, prophets, began to prophesy to the Jews in Judah and Jerusalem in the name of the God of Israel.

Haggai 1:1, 8, On the first day of the sixth month in the second year of Darius the king, the word of the Lord came through Haggai the prophet to the governor of Judah, Zerubbabel, son of Shealtiel, and to the high priest Joshua, son of Jehozadak. Thus says the Lord of hosts: This people has said: "Now is not the time to rebuild the house of the Lord."

Then the word of the Lord came through Haggai the prophet: "Is it time for you to dwell in your paneled houses while this house lies in ruins?" Now says the Lord of hosts:

You have sown much, but have brought in little;
 you have eaten, but have not been satisfied;
You have drunk, but have not become intoxicated;
 you have clothed yourselves, but have not been warmed;

And the hired worker labors for a bag full of holds

Thus says the Lord of hosts:

Reflect on your experience!

Go up into the hill country;
 bring timber, and build the house
That I may be pleased with it,
 and that I may be glorified, says the Lord.
You expected much, but it came to little;
 and what you brought hoe, I blew away.
Why is this?—oracle of the Lord of hosts—
 because my house is the one which lies in ruins,
 while each of you runs to your own house.
Therefore, the heavens withheld the dew,
 and the earth its yield.
And I have proclaimed a devastating heat
 upon the land and upon the mountains,
Upon the grain, the new wine, and the olive oil,
 upon all that the ground brings forth;
Upon human being and beast alike,
 and upon all they produce.

Ezra 5:2, 17, Then the prophets Haggai and Zechariah, son of Iddo, began to prophesy to the Jews in Judah and Jerusalem in the name of the

God of Israel. Thereupon Zerubbabel, son of Shealtiel, and Jeshua, son of Jozadak, began again to build the house of God in Jerusalem, with the prophets of God giving them support. At that time Tattenai, governor of West-of-Euphrates, came to them, along with Shetharbozenai, and their fellow officials, and asked of them: "Who issued the decree for you to build this house and complete this edifice? What are the names of the men who are building this structure?" But the eye of their God was upon the elders of the Jews, and they were not delayed during the time a report went to Darius and a written order came back concerning this matter.

A copy of the letter which Tattenai, governor of West-of-Euphrates, along with Shethar-bozenai and their fellow officials from West-of-Euphrates, sent to King Darius; they sent him a report in which was written the following:

"To King Darius, all good wishes! Let it be known to the king that we have visited the province of Judah and the house of the great God: it is being rebuilt of cut stone and the walls are being reinforced with timber; the work is being carried out diligently, prospering under their hands. We then questioned the elders, addressing to them the following words: 'Who issued the decree for you to build this house and complete this edifice?' We also asked them their names, in order to give you a list of the men who are their leaders. This was their answer to us: 'We are the servants of the God of heaven and earth, and we are rebuilding he house built here many years ago, which a great king of Israel built and completed. But because our ancestors provoked the wrath of the God of heaven, he delivered them into the power of the Chaldean, Nebuchadnezzar, king of Babylon, who destroyed this house and exiled the people to Babylon. King Cyrus issued a decree for the rebuilding of this house of God. Moreover, the gold and silver vessels of the house of God, which Nebuchadnezzar had taken from the temple in Jerusalem and carried off to the temple in Babylon, King Cyrus ordered to be removed from the temple of Babylon, and they were given to a certain Sheshbazzar, whom he named governor. He commanded him: Take these vessels and deposit them in the temple of Jerusalem, and let the house of God be rebuilt on its former site. Then this same Sheshbazzar came and laid the foundations of the house of God in Jerusalem. Since that time to the present the building has been going on and is not yet completed. Now, if it please the king, let a search be made in the royal archives of Babylon to discover whether a decree really was issued to King Cyrus for the rebuilding of this house of God in Jerusalem. And may the king's decision in this matter be communicated to us.

Ezra Chapter 6: 1,16, Thereupon King Darius issued an order to search the archives in which the treasures were stored in Babylon. However, a scroll was found in Ecbatana, the stronghold in the province of Media, containing the following test: "Memorandum. In the first year of his reign, King Cyrus issued a decree: With regard to the house of God in Jerusalem: the house is to be rebuilt as a place for offering sacrifices and bringing burnt offerings. Its height is to be sixty cubits and its width sixty cubits. It shall have three courses of cut stone for each one of timber. The costs are to be borne by the royal house. Also, let the gold and silver vessels of the house of God which Nebuchadnezzar took from the temple of Jerusalem and brought to Babylon be sent back; let them be returned to their place in the temple of Jerusalem and deposited in the house of God."

"Now, therefore, Tattenai, governor of West-of-Euphrates, and Shethar-bozenai and you, their fellow officials in West-of-Euphrates, stay away from there. Let the governor and the elders of the Jews continue the work on that house of God; they are to rebuild it on its former site. I also issue this decree concerning your dealing with these elders of the Jews in the rebuilding of that house of God: Let these men be repaid for their expenses, in full and without delay from the royal revenue, deriving from the taxes of West-of-Euphrates, so that the work not be interrupted. Whatever else is required—young bulls, rams, and lambs for burnt offerings to the God of heaven, wheat, salt, wine, and oil, according to the requirements of the priests who are in Jerusalem—let that be delivered to them day by day without fail, that they may continue to offer sacrifices of pleasing odor to the God of heaven and pray for the life of the king and his sons. I also issue this decree: if any man alters this edict, a beam is to be taken from his house, and he is to be lifted up and impaled on it; and his house is to be reduced to rubble for this offense. And may the God who causes his name to dwell there overthrow every king or people who may undertake to alter this decree or to destroy this house of God in Jerusalem. I, Darius, have issued this decree; let it be diligently executive."

Another situation we find in the bible, is Satan, he was present in the rebuilding of the second temple. He Satan has charges against Israel. In the American Bible Society, the Zechariah 3:1, 7 reads: Then he showed me Joshua the high priest standing before the angel of the Lord, while the adversary stood at his right side to accuse him. And the angel of the Lord said to the adversary, "May the Lord rebuke you, O adversary; may the Lord who has chosen Jerusalem rebuke you! Is this not a brand plucked from the fire?"

Zechariah 2:16, The Lord will inherit Judah as his portion of the holy land, and the Lord will again choose Jerusalem.

Zechariah 3:1, 7,

Adversary; Hebrew Satan, here, the prosecuting attorney, a figure in the Lord's heavenly courtroom. Later tradition understands this figure to be Satan. The filthy garments of Joshua symbolized the guilt of the Israelite people who have become unclean by going into exile. The angel of the Lord purifies the high priest by the removal of his garments. If you walk ... watch over my courts; four components of priestly activity: (1) following God's commandments and teaching them to the people, (2) carrying out cultic functions, (3) participating in the judicial system in certain difficult cases, and (4) administering the laborers and lands in the Temple's domain.

Zechariah 3:1, 7, This is to understand what and why Satan was present in Jerusalem; Satan was opposing the rebuilding of the second temple of the Lord. Meaning, in conflict or competition with a specified or implied subject, differing from or in conflict with each other.

Here is what's going on, Satan vs. the Israelites in a courtroom setting.

Then he showed me Joshua, this is Zechariah's vision (Zechariah had eight visions).

Zechariah 3:1, 7, Then he showed me Joshua the high priest standing before the angel of the Lord, while the adversary stood at his right side to accuse him. And the angel of the Lord said to the adversary, "May the

Lord rebuke you, O adversary; may the Lord who has chosen Jerusalem rebuke you! Is this not a brand plucked from the fire?"

Now Joshua was standing before the angel, clad in filthy garments. Then the angel said to those standing before him. "Remove his filthy garments." And to him he said, "Look, I have taken your guilt from you, and I am clothing you in stately robes. Then he said, "Let them put a clean turban on his head." And they put a clean turban on his head and clothed him with the garments while the angel of the Lord was standing by. Then the angel of the Lord charged Joshua: Thus says the Lord of hosts: If you walk in my ways and carry out my charge, you will administer my house and watch over my courts; and I will give you access to those standing here."

On the St. Michael the Archangel card, we just finished the return of the Israelites back to Jerusalem. They have rebuilt the second temple around (445-432 B.C.)

On the St. Michael the Archangel card we go to God Almighty, Jesus Christ our Savior, and the Angels of the Lord, and St. Michael, who leads the valiant Maccabees to victory.

CHAPTER 9

- We are about to learn about the Maccabee's right now.

Judas Maccabeus, was a Jewish priest, and a son of the priest Mattathias. He led the Maccabean revolt against the Seleucid Empire (167-160 B.C.E.). The Jewish holiday of Hanukkan (Dedication) commemorates the restoration of Jewish worship at the Second Temple in Jerusalem in 164 BCE, after Judas Maccabeus removed all of the statues depicting Greek gods and goddesses and purified it.

Judas is the third son of Mattathias the Hasmonean, a Jewish priest from the village of Modiin. In 167 B.C.E. Mattathias, together with his three sons Judas, Jonathan, Simon and his grandson, John Hyrcanus. Eleazar, although not actually a Maccabee, is celebrated as one of the "Holy Maccabean Martyrs" by the Roman Catholic and Eastern Orthodox churches.

Leadership of Judas Maccabeus, (3:1-9:22)

Leadership of Jonathan, (9:23-12:53)

Leadership of Simon (13:1-16:24)

So, going into 1 Maccabees chapter 1, 1,10, From Alexander the Great to Antiochus Epiphanes.

After Alexander the Macedonian, Philip's son, who came from the land of Kittim, had defeated Darius, king of the Persians and Medes, he became king in his place, having first ruled in Greece. He fought many battles, captured fortresses, and put the kings of the earth to death. He advanced to the ends of the earth, gathering plunder from many nations; the earth fell silent before him, and his heart became proud and arrogant. He collected a very strong army and won dominion over provinces, nations, and rulers, and they paid him tribute.

But after all this he took to his bed, realizing that he was going to die. So he summoned his noblest officers, who had been brought up with him from his youth, and divided his kingdom among them while he was still alive. Alexander had reigned twelve years when he died.

So his officers took over his kingdom, each in his own territory, and after his death they all put on diadems, and so did their sons after them for many years, multiplying evils on the earth.

There sprang from these a sinful offshoot, Antiochus Epiphanes, son of King Antiochus, once a hostage at Rome. He became king in the one hundred and thirty-seventh year of the kingdom of the Greeks.

Alexander the Great served as king of Macedonia, from 336 to 323 B.C. During his time of leadership, he united Greece, and conquered the Persian Empire.

Prophet Daniel was a righteous man of princely lineage and lived about 620-538 B.C. He was carried off to Babylon in 605 B.C. by Nebuchadnezzar.

In Daniel chapter 8, it tells of Daniel's vision of a two-horned ram destroyed by a one-horned goat, followed by the history of the "little horn," which is Daniel's code - word for the Greek King Antiochus IV Epiphanes.

Although set during the reign or regency of King Belshazzar (who probably died in 539 B.C.E.), the subject of the vision is Antiochus' oppression of the Jewish people during the second century B.C.E: he outlawed Jewish customs such as circumcision, the Jewish monthly - Lunar calendar, dietary restrictions, and Sabbath observance, made ownership of the Torah scroll a capital offense, and built an altar to Zeus in the Temple (the abomination of desolation). His program sparked a popular uprising which led to the retaking of Jerusalem and the Temple by Judas Maccabeus (164 BCE.)

Antiochus IV Epiphanes starts on the fifteenth day of the month Kislev, in the year one hundred and forty-five: December 6, 167 B.C. starts the Desolating, abomination.

1 Maccabees 1:56, 63, Any scrolls of the law that they found they tore up and burned. Whoever was found with a scroll of the covenant, and whoever observed the law, was condemned to death by royal decree. So they used their power against Israel, against those who were caught, each month, in the cities. On the twenty-fifth day of each month they sacrificed on the pagan altar that was over the alter of burnt offering, In keeping with the decree, they put to death women who had their children circumcised, and they hung their babies from their necks; their families also and those who had circumcised them were killed.

But many in Israel were determined and resolved in their hearts not to eat anything unclean; they preferred to die rather than to be defiled with food or to profane the holy covenant; and they did die. And very great wrath came upon Israel.

So Antiochus IV Epiphanes is responsible for desolation an abomination, of the temple of the Lord, that started in (167 B.C.).

(1 Maccabees 6:16). The one hundred and forty-ninth year: September 22, (164 B.C. to October 9, 163 B.C.). A Babylonian list of the Seleucid Kings indicates that Antiochus IV Epiphanes died in November or early December of 164, about the same time as the rededication of the Temple.

1 Maccabees 4:36, 61

December 14, 164 B.C.

Days of the dedication: institution of the Feast of Hanukkah, also called the Feast of Dedication (John 10:22, 23). Josephus calls it the Feast of Lights.

John 10:22, 23, The feast of the Dedication was then taking place in Jerusalem. It was winter. And Jesus walked about in the temple area on the Portico of Solomon.

This would have been around the time of Jesus Christ' Birthday, December 25th.

December 25

The Virgin Mary, pregnant with the Son of God, gave birth to Jesus nine months later on the winter solstice. From Rome, the Christ's Nativity Celebration spread to other Christian churchs to the west and east, and soon most Christians were celebrating Christ's birth on December 25.

Solstice meaning?

What are the two types of Solstice?
1) June Solstice, occurs in June 21 and also known as the Northern Solstice.
2) December Solstice, occurs in December 21 and also known as the Southern Solstice.

What happens to the sun on December 25?

The sun stops moving south at least perceivably for 3 days and during this 3-day pause, the sun resides in the vicinity of the southern cross, or crux constellation and after time, on December 25th, the sun moves 1 degree this time north. Foreshadowing longer days, warmth, and spring.

Going back to 1st Maccabees 4:36, 61

Purification and Rededication of the Temple.

Then Judas Maccabeus and his brothers said, "Now that our enemies have been crushed, let us go up to purify the sanctuary and rededicate it." So the whole army assembled, and and went up to Mount Zion. They found the sanctuary desolate, the altar desecrated, the gates burnt, weeds growing in the courts as in a thicket or on some mountain, and the priests' chambers demolished. Then they tore their garments and made great lamentation; they sprinkled their heads with ashes and prostrated themselves. And when the signal was given with trumpets, they cried out to Heaven.

Judas appointed men to attack those in the citadel, while he purified the sanctuary. He chose blameless priests, devoted to the law; these purified the sanctuary and carried away the stones of the defilement to an unclean place. They deliberated what ought to be done with the altar for burnt offerings that had been desecrated. They decided it best to tear it down, lest it be a lasting shame to them that the Gentiles had defiled it; so they tore down the altar. They stored the stones in a suitable place on the temple mount, until the coming of a prophet who could determine what to do with them. Then they took uncut stones, according to the law, and built a new altar like the former one. They also repaired the sanctuary and the interior of the temple and consecrated the courts. They made new sacred vessels and brought the lampstand, the altar of incense, and the table into the temple. Then they burned incense on the altar and lighted the lamps on the lampstand, and these illuminated the temple. They also put loaves on the table and hung up the curtains. Thus they finished all the work they had undertaken.

They rose early on the morning of the twenty-fifth day of the ninth month, that is, the month of Kislev, in the year one hundred and forty-eight, and offered sacrifice according to the law on the new altar for burnt offering that they had made. On the anniversary of the day on which the Gentiles had desecrated it, on that very day it was rededicated with songs, harps lyres, and cymbals. All the people prostrated themselves and adored and praised Heaven, who had given them success.

For eight days they celebrated the dedication of the altar and joyfully offered burnt offerings and sacrifices of deliverance and praise. They ornamented the facade of the temple with gold crowns and shields; they repaired the gates and the priests chambers and furnished them with doors. There was great joy among the people now that the disgrace brought by the Gentiles was removed. Then Judas and his brothers and the entire assembly of Israel decreed that every year for eight days, from the twenty-fifth day of the month Kislev, the days of the dedication of the altar should be observed with joy and gladness on the anniversary.

At that time they built high walls and strong towers around Mount Zion, to prevent the Gentiles from coming and trampling it as they had done before. Judas also placed a garrison there to protect it, and likewise fortified Beth-zur, that the people might have a stronghold facing Idumea.

To make any sense of what's going on here, we are going to have to read Daniel chapter 8. The Ram and the He-goat. Daniels vision.

The two-horned ram represents the combined kingdom of the Medes and Persians, destroyed by Alexander's Hellenistic Empire originating in the west. Once again the author is interested only in the Seleucid dynasty, which emerged from the dissolution of Alexander's empire after his death in (323 B.C.).

The He-goat being Alexander the Great grew very powerful, but at the height of its strength the great horn was shattered, and in its place came up four others, facing the four winds of heaven. Out of one of them came a little horn.

Daniel 8:8, and in its place came up four others. 1 Maccabees 1:8, so his officers took over his kingdom (meaning Alexander the Great).

Daniel 8:9 - Out of one of them came a little horn. In 1 Maccabees 1:8, 10 out of the officers of Alexander the Great, there sprang from these a sinful offshoot, Antiochus IV Epiphanes. This little horn of Daniel 8:9 - s Antiochus IV Epiphanes.

So I will continue with Daniel chapter 8:9 all the way to Daniel chapter 8:27 - this could explain who is behind this situation. So far we are looking at 3 years of abomination of Desolating the Temple of the Lord in 167 B.C. to 164 B.C. by the little horn, Antiochus IV Epiphanes.

Out of one of them came a little horn which grew and grew toward the south, the east, and the glorious land. It grew even to the host of heaven, so that it cast down to earth some of the host and some of the stars and trampled on them. It grew even to the Prince of the host, from whom the daily sacrifice was removed, and whose sanctuary was cast down. The host was given over together with the daily sacrifice in the course of transgression. It cast truth to the ground and was succeeding in its undertaking.

I heard a holy one speaking, and another said to whichever one it was that spoke, "How long shall the events of this vision last concerning the daily sacrifice, the desolating sin," the giving over of the sanctuary and the host for trampling?" He answered him,

"For two thousand three hundred evening and mornings; then the sanctuary shall be set right."

Before I continue, I want to go back to Daniel chapter 8:10, 12 - The commentary, it reads:

The he-goat grew very powerful, but at the height of its strength the great horn was shattered, and in its place came up four others, facing the four winds of heaven. Out of one of them came a little horn which grew and grew toward the south, the east, and the glorious land. IT grew even to the host of heaven, so that it cast down to earth some of the host and some of the stars and trampled on them.

1 Maccabees 1:44, 50, The king sent letters by messenger to Jerusalem and to the cities of Judah, ordering them to follow customs foreign to their land.

Antiochus IV Epiphanes, (Greek: God Manifest) also called Antiochus Epiphanes (the mad), (born c. 215 BC - died 164, Tabae, Iran), Seleucid King of the Hellenistic Syrian Kingdom who reigned from 175 to 164 BC. As a ruler he was best known for his encouragement of Greek culture and institutions.

This is that king who sent letters by messenger to Jerusalem. The letter reads, to prohibit burnt offerings, sacrifices, and libations in the sanctuary, to profane the Sabbaths and feast days, to desecrate the sanctuary and the sacred ministers, to build pagan altars and temples and shrines, to sacrifice swine and unclean animals, to leave their sons uncircumcised and to defile themselves with every kind of impurity and abomination; so that they might forget the law and change all its ordinances. Whoever refused to act according to the command of the king was to be put to death.

OK going to Daniel 8:14 again, "For two thousand three hundred evening and mornings then the sanctuary shall be set right."

When you do the numbers on 2,300 evenings and mornings, it comes out to 6 years and 4 months.

So, we know that the desolating, abomination that Antiochus IV Epiphanes starts in 167 B.C. and ends in 164 B.C. when he dies.

The first abomination of desolation lasts 3 years.

Then at the same time in 164 B.C. 1 Maccabees chapter 4:36, The Purification and Rededication of the Temple.

Then Judas and his brothers said, "Now that our enemies have been crushed, let us go up to purify the sanctuary and rededicate it."

Daniel chapter 8 says in verse 14, "For two thousand three hundred evening and morning; then the sanctuary shall be set right."

That leaves three and a half years. The numbers on two thousand three hundred evening and morning, we have three years of abomination of desolation by Antiochus IV Epiphanes. That leaves three years and four months for the next transgression of desolation of both the sanctuary host to be trampled underfoot? At that time a lamb was sacrificed twice daily, meaning, it was done, morning and evening, on the altar of the Jewish temple in Jerusalem.

So now we are looking for the next three and a half years of the transgression of desolation.

Daniel 9:26, 27, "After the sixty-two weeks an anointed one shall be cut down, with no one to help him. and the people of a leader who will come, shall destroy the city and the sanctuary. His end shall come in a flood; until the end of the war, which is decreed, there will be desolation. For one week he shall abolish sacrifice and offering; in their place shall be the desolating abomination until the ruin that is decreed is poured out upon the desolator"

The flood is a flood of unstoppable war and violence, as described in Isaiah 59:19: Those in the west shall fear the name of the Lord, and those in the east, his glory, coming like a pent-up stream driven on by the breath of the Lord.

In 63 CE the Romans captured Jerusalem and Judea became an outpost of the Roman Empire, but in 66 CE the Jews rose in revolt against the Romans as their ancestors had once done against Antiochus IV Epiphanes. The resulting first Jewish-Roman war ended in 70 CE when the legions of the Roman General Titus surrounded and eventually captured Jerusalem, the city and the temple were razed to the ground, and the only habitation on the site until the first third of the next century was a Roman military camp.

The Son of Emperor Vespasian Was Prince Titus

In 70 A.D. God executed judgement upon Jerusalem just as Jesus had forewarned 40 years earlier with the statement about the destruction of the temple, and there shall not be left one stone upon another (Matt 24:2). In 66 A.D. the Roman armies had surrounded the city and then mysteriously pulled back. This was the warning Jesus gave to His followers: "When you see Jerusalem surrounded by armies, know that its desolation is at hand." Luke 21:20. At this time, the Believers left the city as instructed by Jesus, let them which are in Judea flee to the mountains. The unbelievers stayed in the city and received the judgment of God at the hands of Prince Titus and the Romans armies.

This doesn't sound like to me that the Prince Titus was in any way the antichrist.

According to Daniel 9:26, both stories go together first you have: after the sixty-two weeks an anointed one shall be cut down with no one to help him.

Matthew 27:50, But Jesus cried out again in a loud voice, and yielded up his spirit.

And the people of the prince who is to come shall 'destroy' the city and the sanctuary. The end of it shall be with a flood, and till the end of the war desolations are determined. The Prince is Titus, this is not the transgression of desolation we are looking for.

But Daniel 9:27 is the second transgression of desolation that is lasting three and a half years and it reads: "For one week he shall make a firm covenant with the many; half the week he shall abolish sacrifice and offering; in their place shall be the desolating abomination until the ruin that is decreed is poured out upon the desolator."

Daniel 8:13, 14, I heard a holy one speaking, and another said to whichever one it was that spoke, "How long shall the events of this vision last concerning the daily sacrifice, the desolating sin," the giving over of the sanctuary and the host for trampling?" He answered them, "For two thousand three hundred evenings and mornings; then the sanctuary shall be set right."

According to Revelations 11:1, 2, Then I was given a measuring rod like a staff and I was told, "Come and measure the temple of God and the altar, and count those who are worshiping in it. But exclude the outer court of the temple; do not measure it, for it has been handed over to the Gentiles, who will trample the holy city for forty-two months.

2 Thessalonians 2:1, 12, We ask you, brothers, with regard to the coming of our Lord Jesus Christ and our assembling with him, not to be shaken out of your minds suddenly, or to be alarmed either by a "spirit" or by an oral statement, or by a letter allegedly from us to the effect that the day of the Lord is at hand. Let no one deceive you in any way. For unless the apostasy comes first and the lawless one is revealed, the one doomed to perdition, who opposes and exalts himself above every so-called God and object of worship, so as to seat himself in the temple of God, claiming that he is a god—do you not recall that while I was still with you I told you these things? And now you know what is restraining, that he may be revealed at this time. For the mystery of lawlessness is already at work. But the one

who restrains is to do so only for the present, until he is removed from the scene. And then the lawless one will be revealed, whom the Lord Jesus will kill with the breath of his mouth and ender powerless by the manifestation of his coming, the one whose coming springs from the power of Satan in every might deed and in signs and wonders that lie, and in every wicked deceit for those who are perishing because they have not accepted the love of truth so that they may be saved. Therefore, God is sending them a deceiving power so that they may believe the lie, that all who have not believed the truth but have approved wrongdoing may be condemned.

In 1 Thessalonians 4:16, 17, For the Lord himself, with a word of command, with the voice of an archangel and with the trumpet of God, will come down from heaven, and the dead in Christ will rise first. Then we who are alive, who are left, will be caught up together with them in the clouds to meet the Lord in the air. Thus we shall always be with the Lord. Therefore, console one another with these words.

Sounds like the rapture of the church, and the great tribulation, and the last seven years. The first 3½ years, anti-Christ is the beast, and then there's the false prophet. Then Satan the second 3½ years.

In Revelation 13:4, 7, They worshiped the dragon because it gave its authority to the beast; they also worshiped the beast and said, "Who can compare with the beast or who can fight against it?"

The beast was given a mouth uttering proud boasts and blasphemies, and it was given authority to act for forty-two months. IT opened its mouth to utter blasphemies against God, blaspheming his name and his dwelling and those who dwell in heaven.

42 months is 3 and a half years, this is Satan and the antichrist.

Another place in the bible where you will find 3½ years, is in Daniel 7:23, 27.

The fourth beast shall be a fourth kingdom on earth, different from all the others; the whole earth it shall devour, trample down and crush. The ten horns shall be ten kings rising out of that kingdom; another shall rise up after them, who shall lay low three kings. He shall speak against the Most High and wear down the holy one of the Most High, intending to change the feast days and the law. They shall be handed over to him for a time, two times, and half a time. But when the court is convened, and his dominion is taken away to be abolished and completely destroyed, then the kingship and dominion and majesty of all the kingdoms under the heavens shall be given to the people of the holy ones of the Most High, whose kingship shall be an everlasting kingship, whom all dominions shall serve and obey.

Revelation 13:16, 18 reads: It forced all the people, small and great, rich and poor, free and slave, to be given a stamped image on their right hands or their foreheads, so that no one could buy or sell except one who had the stamped image of the beast's name or the number that stood for its name.

Wisdom is needed here; one who understands can calculate the number of the beast, for it is a number that stands for a person. His number is six hundred and sixty-six.

So, the next question is did the papacy really uproot the horns of Daniel 7:8, 24, 25.

The Vandals, Ostrogoths, and the Heruli's are the three kings uprooted.

The Vandals were Arian Christians, while the Romans were Trinitarian (or Nicean) Christians. Religious differences caused problems between the Vandels and the Romans, but these were forgotten, temporarily, in the invasion of the region by the Huns.

The Ostrogoths and the Visigoths, first appear in history living in the area around the around the black sea. They made constant incursions against the provinces of Rome and proved a resilient and perpetual nuisance to the Empire until the invasion of the Huns in 375 CE. A large portion of the populace (according to some sources, 200,000) fled the area to seek the protection of the Roman Empire under the Emperor Valens (364-378 CE) and these people became known as the Visigoths. The rest of the people remained, enduring the rule of the Huns, but retaining a certain degree of autonomy.

After the death of Attila the Hun in 453 CE and the dissolution of his empire, the Ostrogoths declared their independence. Eventually, under Theodoric the Great, they migrated and settled in Italy. Theodoric established the Ostrogoths Empire but his successors came into conflict with the Byzantine Empire which sent the General Flavius Belisarius (l. 505-565 CE) to bring the back in line in accordance with Byzantine interests. The last great Gothic King Totila (r. 541-552 CE) led the Goth resistance against the Byzantines and, after his death in (553 CE), the Ostrogoths lost their autonomy and ethnic identity, merging with the people of Italy, the Lombards, and dispersing into the regions of modern-day France and Germany.

The Goths - those who would eventually be known as Ostrogoths and Visigoths - probably originated around the area of Gdansk, Poland before they began migrating to the regions of modern-day Germany and Hungary.

Who destroyed the Heruli's? The Heruli's were a subject tribe of the Goths and their later Ostrogoths divion until the latter were destroyed by the Huns in 375. Like a great many tribes in Eastern Europe they were subjugated by the Huns until the death of Attila, after which they re-emerged along with a branch of the Goths.

The Heruli's were defeated again (267 A.D.) by the Emperor Claudius II Gothicus. They raided towns in the Roman Empire, scoring their greatest success in AD 267, when they captured Byzantium and sacked Greek cities. Two years later, the eastern Heruli were crushingly defeated by the Roman Emperor Claudius II Gothicus in a battle near Naissus (modern Nis Yugos).

The only time you hear a Pope getting involved is when a meeting was set between Pope Leo and Attila the Hun.

In 452, Attila the Hun led an army to attack Rome. In order to protect the vulnerable city, Pope Leo met with Attila. It is unclear exactly what was said between the two leaders. What we do know is that at the end of the meeting. Attila and his army departed, leaving Rome untouched.

Confronting Attila the Hun or any other barbarian army was not in his job description ... Pope Leo, some of the biggest headaches came from his brother bishops ... To pay off the debt of our state. To pay Attila the Hun.

Attila the Hun was the leader of the Hunnic Empire from 434 to 453 A.D. Also ... the Romans Empire agreed to pay Attila and Bleda 700 pounds of gold a year. Emperor Valentinian III refused but Attila was not one to give up.

The second time you hear a Pope getting involved. The Lombards, what religion were the Lombards? Initially the Lombards were Arian Christians or pagans, which put them at odds with the Roman population as well as the Byzantine Empire and the Pope. However, by the end of the 7th century, their conversion to Catholicism was all but complete.

Where did the Lombards originate from? The Lombards were a Germanic tribe that originated in Scandinavia and migrated to the region of Pannonia roughly modern-day Hungary).

What language did the Lombards speak? West German language that was spoken by the Lombards, the German people who settled in Italy in the sixth century. It was already declining by the seventh century because the invaders quickly adopted the Latin, spoken by the local population.

The Lombard -vs- The Pope

The Siege or Battle of Pavia was fought in 773-774 in northern Italy, near Ticinum (modern Pavia), and resulted in the victory of the Franks under Charlemagne against the Lombards under King Desiderius. Charlemagne, had succeeded to the throne in 768 jointly with his brother Carloman. At the time there was antagonism between not only the two ruling brothers, but between the King of the Lombards, Desiderius, and the papacy. In 772, Pope Hadrian I expelled all the Lombard officials from the papal curia. In response, Desiderius invaded papal territory, even taking Otriculum (modern Otricoli), just a day's march from Rome. Hadrian the Pope, called Charlemagne for assistance.

Charles had produced an alliance with the Lombards by marrying one of Desiderius' daughters. Desiderata; within a year, however, he had changed his mind about the marriage and alliance, and divorced his wife, sending her back to her father. This was taken as an insult by the Lombards. Upon the death of Carloman in 771, his own wife, Gerberge, fled the kingdom with her children for reasons now unclear. (Einhard disingenuously protests that she spurned her husband's brother for no reason at all) and sought refuge with Desiderius at Pavia. Desiderius now returned the insult to the Franks by giving her asylum, and protesting that her children be allowed their share of the kingdom of the Franks. The relationship between Frank and Lombard now broke down completely and the Pope took full advantage. His embassy landed at Marseilles and traveled to Thionville, where they delivered this message: To Charlemagne.

They (the Lombards) would attack us (the Pope) by land and water, conquer the city of Rome and lead ourselves into captivity ... Therefore we implore you by the living God and the Prince of the Apostles to hasten to our aid immediately, lest we be destroyed.

Charlemagne ascertained the truth of Desiderius aggressions and the threat he posed to his own Frankish realm and marched his troops towards Italy in the early summer of 773.

The Siege

Charles army had 10.000-40,000 troops, he divided it in half, giving command of one half to his uncle, Bernard, son of Charles Martel, and led it through the Alpine passes; he through that of the Dora Susa near Mont Cenis, and Bernard through the Great St Bernard Pass. At the foot of the mountains, Charle's army met the fortification of Desiderius, but scouting forces found an alternate route. A cavalcade was sent to attack the defenders from the flank and, with Bernard's forces approaching from the east, the Lombards fled to fortified Pavia. The Frankish troops then marched on to begin the siege of Pavia by September. The entire Frankish army was capable of wholly surrounding the Lombard capital, however they had brought no siege engines. The Lombards too had failed in their preparations; the city was poorly stocked with food and the surrounding country side was now in the hands of the Franks, Desiderius remained in Pavia, but Adelchis, his son, had left to stronger Verona to guard over the family of Carloman's family were taken. Charles then began to subdue the whole region around Pavia in the early months of 774. Charles even visited the Pope in Rome at Easter. No other Lombard dukes or counts made any attempt at relief and Desiderius made no strong counter attack. In the tenth month of the siege, famine was hitting Pavia hard and Desiderius, realising that he was left on his own, opened the gates to Charles and surrendered on some Tuesday in June.

The Lombards who managed to leave Pavia crossed the Apennines and settled in present in present-day Liguria where the Republic of Genoa was born later.

Legacy

After the victory, Charlemagne had himself declared Rex Langobardorum, and from that time onwards he was to be called King of the Franks and Lombards. This unique history of the of the German kingdoms of the dark ages: a ruler taking the title of the conquered Charles was forging what could truly be called an empire. He was also allying himself very closely with the church as its protector. His recognition of temporal papal authority in central Italy laid the foundation for Medieval Papal Power. The decline of the Lombard state had been swift and the changes wrought in Italy by the Frankish conquest were great. Many Franks entered into positions of power and authority in Italy, though many Lombards, on account of their willingness to make peace with Charles, retained their positions. As Paul K. Davis writes, The defeat and consequent destruction of the Lombard monarchy rid Rome of its most persistent threat to papal security, laying the ground work for the Holy Roman Empire, and the Church of Jesus Christ.

Matthew 16:13, 19, When Jesus went into the region of Caesarea Philippi he asked his disciples, "Who do people say that the Son of Man is?" They replied, "Some say John the Baptist, others Elijah, still others Jeremiah or one of the prophets." He said to them, "But who do you say that I am?" Simon Peter said in reply, "You are the Messiah, the Son of the living God." Jesus said to him in reply, "Blessed are you, Simon son of Jonah. For flesh and blood has not revealed this to you, but my heavenly Father. And so I say to you, you are Peter, and upon this rock I will build my church, and the gates of the netherworld shall not prevail against it. I will give you the keys to the kingdom of heaven. Whatever you bind on earth shall be bound in heaven; and whatever you loose on earth shall be loosed in heaven."

John 21:15, 19, When they had finished breakfast, Jesus said to Simon Peter, "Simon, son of John, do you love me more than these?" He said to him, "Yes, Lord, you know that I love you." HE said to him, "Feed my lambs." He then said to him a second time, "Simon, son of John, do you love me?" He said to him, "Yes, Lord, you know that I love you." He said to him, "Tend my sheep." He said to him the third time, "Simon, son of John, do you love me?" Peter was distressed that he had said to him a third time, "Do you love me?" and he said to him, "Lord, you know everything; you know that I love you." Jesus said to him, "Feed my sheep. Amen, amen, I say to you, when you were younger, you used to dress yourself and go where you wanted; but when you grow old, you will stretch out your hands, and someone else will dress you and lead you where you do not want to go. He said this signifying by what kind of death he would glorify God. And when he had said this, he said to him, "Follow me."

Jesus prediction of Peter's death. The narrator interprets this as referring to Peter's martyrdom (John 21:19)

Why Nero Goes Down as One of the Worst Villains in History ... According to ancient tradition, Peter and Paul both died during this first official Roman persecution of the Christians. Peter was crucified (upside down).

Nero isn't just a sinner who made the wrong choice: in much of Christian legend, and even theology, he is literally the Antichrist.

And that raised Nero to a higher position than anyone else in the pantheon of Christian persecutors. He wasn't just a bad man: for many Christians, Nero was the anti-Christ himself.

How late did Nero legends survive? No one can really tell; they were legends passed down among the ordinary illiterate people. But in the year 1099, more than a thousand years after Nero died, we get a hint that they were still circulating. In that year, Pope Paschal II built what is now the church of Santa Maria at the Piazza del Popolo in Rome. It was built on what was believed to be the site of Nero's tomb, and the Pope built it specifically to exorcise Nero's ghost.

So, Nero died at the age of thirty, after a turbulent 13-year reign, the Roman senate ran out of patience and declared Nero a public enemy. Nero then fled, and on June 9, 68 A.D., at the age of 30, he committed suicide. His death ended the Julio-Claudian dynasty.

Flavia Julia Helena or Saint Helena was the mother of Roman Emperor Constantine the Great, went to great pains to build the basilica on the site of Saint Peter's grave, and this influenced the layout of the building. Old St. Peter's Basilica was the building that stood, from the 4th to 16th centuries, where the new St. Peter Basilica stands today in the Vatican City. Construction of the basilica, built over the historical site of the Circus of Nero, began during the reign of Emperor Constantine I. The name Old St. Peter's Basilica has been used since the construction of the current basilica to distinguish the two building.

Since the crucifixion and burial of Saint Peter in 64 A.D., the spot was thought to be the location of the tomb of Saint Peter, where there stood a small shrine. The structure was filled with tombs and bodies of Saints and Popes. Bones continued to be found in construction.

Constantine the Great, was a Roman Emperor from 306 to 337, he is the son of Flavius Constantius.

How to see the Pope in Rome - best visit time, updated for 2020.

How can I meet the Pope in the Vatican City?

To see the Pope in Rome, who is Pope Francis, you have three options. The first option is to visit on a Sunday morning just before noon for a chance to see him for free. You can also get a papal audience ticket in St. Peter's Square, Nervi auditorium or a ticket to the Vatican Hall.

This proves that the Papacy did not uproot three kings in Daniel seven verse 24. The Ten Kings was a plot to destroy the papacy in Rome but failed. Half of these kings converted to Christianity.

Daniel 7:25, He shall speak against the Most High and wear down the holy one of the Most High, intending to change the feast days and the law. They shall be handed over to him for a time, two times, and half a time. That's the second half of the transgression of desolation. Daniel 8:13, 14 again, says: I heard a holy one speaking, and another said to whichever one it was that spoke, "How long shall the events of this vision last concerning the daily sacrifice, the desolating sin," the giving over of the sanctuary and the host for trampling? He answered him, "For two thousand three hundred evenings and mornings; then the sanctuary shall be set right. The first abomination was with Antiochus IV Epiphanes 3 yrs. And the second is the second half of the Great tribulation, that's two thousand three hundred days, 6 and a half years, really 6 years and 4 months.

Antiochus IV Epiphanes was a form of the antichrist.

Just like Emperor Nero, he also was a form of the antichrist.

There are many more leaders who play the role of the antichrist and killed thousands of Christians.

1 John 4:3, and every spirit that does not acknowledge Jesus does not belong to God. This is the spirit of the antichrist that, as you heard is to come, but in fact is already in the world.

The Great Tribulation is 7 years and this occurs following the rapture of the church.

2 Thessalonians 2:1, We ask you, brothers, with regard to the coming of our Lord Jesus Christ and our assembling with him.

Rapture of the church, then the Great Tribulation, a 7-year period. 3½ years Antichrist is the beast, there is a false prophet, and the second abomination and desolation. In Jerusalem by Satan himself for the last 3½ years. Then Jesus Christ comes to destroy the Antichrist beast, the false prophet, and Satan goes to prison for a thousand years.

2 Thessalonians 2:8, 9, And then the lawless one will be revealed, whom the Lord Jesus will kill with the breath of his mouth and render powerless by the manifestation of his coming, the one who is coming springs from the power of Satan in every mighty deed and in signs and wonders that lie.

Same in Daniel 7:25, 26, The second abomination in the third temple for 3½ years. Then the saints shall be given into his hands, meaning Satan, for a time and times and half a time, 3½ years. Then Daniel 7:26, Jesus Christ comes to destroy Satan works.

Verse 26, 27, But when the court is convened, and his dominion is taken away to be abolished and completely destroyed, then the kingship and dominion and majesty of all the kingdoms under the heavens shall be given to the people of the holy one of the Most High, whose kingship shall be an everlasting kingship, whom all dominions shall serve and obey.

Revelation 13:5, 6 says the same thing: three and a half. The beast was given a mouth uttering proud boasts and blasphemies, and it was given authority to act for forty-two months. It opened its mouth to utter blasphemies against God, blaspheming his name and his dwelling and those who dwell in heaven.

Revelation 13:16, 17, It forced all people, small and great, rich and poor, free and slave, to be given a stamped image on their right hands or their foreheads, so tht no one could buy or sell except one who had the stamped image of the beast's name or the number that stood for its name.

Revelation 19:16, He has a name written on his cloak and on his thigh,

King of kings
And Lord of lords

Revelations 19:17, 21, Then I saw an angel sanding on the sun. He cried out in a loud voice to all the birds flying high overhead, "Come here. Gather for God's great feast, to eat the flesh of kings, the flesh of military officers, and the flesh of warriors, the flesh of horses and of their riders, and the flesh of all, free and slave, small and great." Then I saw the beast and the kings of the earth and their armies gathered to fight against the one riding the horse and against his army. The beast was caught and with it the false prophet who had performed in its sight the signs by which he led astray those who had accepted the mark of the beast and those who had worshiped its image. The two were thrown alive into the fiery pool burning with sulfur. The rest were killed by the sword that came out of the mouth of the one riding the horse, and all the birds gorged themselves on their flesh.

In Revelation 20:1, 10, Then I saw an angel come down from heaven, holding in his hand the key to the abyss and a heavy chain. He seized the dragon, the ancient serpent, which is the Devil or Satan, and tied it up for a thousand years and threw it into the abyss, which he locked over it and sealed, so that it could no longer lead the nations astray until the thousands years was completed. After this, it is to be released for a short time.

Then I saw thrones; those who sat on them were entrusted with judgment. I also saw the souls of those who had been beheaded for their witness to Jesus and for the word of God, and who had not worshiped the beast or its image nor had accepted its mark on their foreheads or hands. They came to life and they reigned with Christ for a thousand years. The rest of the dead did not come to life until the thousand years were over. This is the first resurrection. Blessed and holy is the one who shares in the first resurrection. The second death has no power over these; they will be priests of God and of Christ, and they will reign with him for the thousand years.

When the thousand years are completed, Satan will be released from his prison. HE will go out to deceive the nations at the four corners of the earth, Gog and Magog, to gather them for battle; their number is like the sand of the sea. They invaded the breadth of the earth and surrounded the camp of the holy ones and the beloved city. But fire came down from heaven and consumed them. The Devil who had led them astray was thrown into the pool of fire and sulfur, where the beast and the false prophet were. There they will be tormented day and night forever and ever.

With a cherub I placed you; I put you on the holy mountain of God, where you walked among fiery stones. Ezekiel 28:14. Now Satan, he rebelled against God, the beast antichrist, and the false prophet are all fallen angels. So, the first and second abomination of desolation, Antiochus IV Epiphanes is the first, and the beast the antichrist, and false prophet, then Satan the last abomination of desolation.

This ends the story of Judas Maccabeus and his family who was victorious over the Greeks and won Jerusalem back.

This was the prayer of Judas Maccabeus, II Maccabees 15:21, 24.

The Defeat of Nicanor. Verses 21 to 24, Maccabeus, surveying the hosts before him, the variety of weaponry, and the fierceness of their beasts, stretched out his hands toward heaven and called upon the Lord who works wonders; for he knew that it is not weapons but the Lord's decision that brings victory to those who deserve it. Calling upon God, he spoke in this manner: "You, master, sent your angel in the days of King Hezekiah of Judea, and he slew a hundred and eighty-five thousand men of Sennacherib's camp. And now, Sovereign of the heavens, send a good angel to spread fear and trembling ahead of us. By the might of your arm may those be struck down who have blasphemously come against your holy people! With these words he ended his prayer.

You can find this story in 2 Kings 19:14, 37, Hezekiah's prayer was answered by God Almighty. Now Judas Maccabeus prays the same prayer. And now, sovereign of the heavens, send a good angel to spread fear and trembling ahead of us. By the might of your arm may those be struck down who have blasphemously come against your holy people! With these words he ended his prayer.

Nicanor and his troops advanced to the sound of trumpets and battle songs. But Judas and his troops met the enemy with supplication and prayers. Fighting with their hands and praying to God with their hearts, they laid low at least thirty-five thousand, and rejoiced greatly over this manifestation of God's power. When the battle was over and they were joyfully departing, they discovered Nicanor fallen there in all his armor; so they raised tumultuous shouts in their ancestral language in praise of the divine Sovereign.

St. Michael the Archangel was present in leading the valiant Maccabees to victory and defends us in battle.

CHAPTER 10

The story of St. Michael the Archangel, who rescues the body of Moses from the envious grasp of the Evil one, Satan himself.

Jude 1:9, Speaks of an occasion when St. Michael the Archangel, in contending with Satan, when he disputed about the body of Moses. Apparently, there was a contention over the body of Moses, and according to Jude 1:9, Yet the archangel Michael, when he argued with the devil in a dispute over the body of Moses, did not venture to pronounce a reviling judgment upon him but said, "May the Lord rebuke you!" Yet why Michael contended with Satan over the body of Moses is less clear.

Some say that the devil wanted to use Moses' body as an object of worship to lead Israel astray into idolatry. Others think that Satan want to desecrate the body of Moses and claimed a right to it because Moses had murdered an Egyptian.

But consider that God had another purpose for Moses' body, which Satan wanted to defeat: Moses appears in bodily form with Elijah (whose body was caught up to heaven (2 Kings 2) at the Transfiguration (Matthew 17:1, 3) and perhaps Moses and Elijah are the two witnesses of Revelation 11. Another person was Enoch, (Genesis 5:23, 24) The whole lifetime of Enoch was three hundred and sixty-five years. Enoch walked with God, and he was no longer here, for God took him.

Apparently, God had a purpose to fulfill with the body of Moses before the time of general resurrection, so God made special provision to bury the body of Moses Himself. And, perhaps, God preserved the body of Moses in some way. God wanted to protect the body of Moses, so no one knows the whereabouts of his grave to this day. Seemingly, they searched for it (as would be expected) out of a desire to memorialize this great leader of the nation.

Moses was one hundred and twenty years old when he died: Moses' life was neatly divided into thirds. He spent 40 years as the crown prince of Egypt, 40 years as a humble shepherd in the wilderness, and 40 years leading the children of Israel to their destiny in the Promised Land. The first two-thirds were in preparation for the last one third. Moses was willing to let God prepare him for 80 years.

His eyes were not dim nor his natural vigor abated: This confirmed what was observed at Deuteronomy 31:1 (I can no longer go out and come in). Moses was not hindered by physical infirmity, but by the command of God.

The children of Israel wept ... the days of weeping and mourning for Moses ended. As great as Moses was, the days of mourning for him ended. It was time to move on. God's program did not end with Moses, nor does it end with any man. The torch is passed, and God's work goes on.

The legacy of Moses.

Joshua's leadership in Israel.

Now Joshua the son of Nun was full of the spirit of wisdom, for Moses had laid his hands on him; so the children of Israel heeded him, and did as the Lord had commanded Moses.

For Moses had laid his hands on him: Moses' prayer for Joshua was answered. Joshua was indeed full of the spirit of wisdom. Best of all, the children of Israel heeded him. The real test of leadership is to see if people actually follow you.

The unique legacy of Moses.

But since then there has not arisen in Israel a prophet like Moses, whom the Lord knew face to face, in all the signs and wonders which the Lord sent him to do in the land of Egypt, before Pharaoh, before all his servants, and in all his land, and by all that mighty power and all the great terror which Moses performed in the sight of all Israel.

Since then there has not arisen in Israel a prophet like Moses:

Joshua was a capable leader for Israel, and God's work went on, but that did not diminish Moses unique legacy.

Since then there has not arisen in Israel a prophet like Moses: Several things made Moses unique.

Whom the Lord knew face to face: Moses was unique because of his personal intimacy with God. The term face to face does not literally mean physical face to physical face, but it has the idea of free and unhindered communication. Moses had a remarkably intimate relationship with God.

All the signs and wonders which the Lord sent him to do: Moses was unique in the number and kind of miraculous works he was associated with.

All that mighty power and all the great terror which Moses performed: Moses was unique in the power and authority with which he led the nation of Israel.

Since then there has not arisen in Israel a prophet like Moses:

There were greater rulers over Israel than Moses, greater leaders, greater prophets, and greater priests. But before the coming of Jesus Christ the Messiah, there was never one man who held all offices so gloriously as Moses did.

In him were concentrated all the offices of Israel - prophet, ruler, judge and priest. If some who held these offices were great, Moses was the greatest of them all.

Next one on the list of St. Michael card is: And since Christ's coming, the church has ever venerated St. Michael as her special patron and protector.

Saint Michael in the Catholic Church is viewed as the commander of the Army of God. From the time of the apostles, he has been invoked and honored as the protector of the church. Scripture describes him as "One of the Chief Princes" and the leader of heaven's forces in their triumph over the powers of hell.

What does St. Michael protect you from?

Saint Michael the Archangel: Defend us in battle. Be our protection against the wickedness and snares of the devil; may God rebuke him, we humbly pray; and do thou, O Prince of the Heavenly Host, by the power of God, thrust into hell Satan and all evil spirits who wander through the world for the ruin of souls Amen."

What does St. Michael help with?

His first role is the leader of the Army of God and the leader of heaven's forces in their triumph over the powers of hell. He is viewed as the angelic model for the virtues of the spiritual warrior, with the conflict against evil at times viewed as the battle within.

Ephesians 6:12 reads, For our struggle is not with flesh and blood, but with the principalities, with the powers, with the world rulers of this present darkness, and with the evil spirits in the heavens.

Now we go to the next reading:

She invokes him by name in her confession of sin.

The Catholic Church teaches that sacramental confession requires three "acts" on the part of the penitent: contrition (sorrow of the soul for the sins committed), disclosure of the sins (the confession) and satisfaction (the penance, doing something to make amends for the sins.).

What are the 5 steps of confession?
- Examine your conscience.
- Be sincerely sorry for your sins.
- Confess your sins.
- Resolve to amend your life.
- After your confession to the penance that your priest assigns.

1 John 1:9, 10, If we acknowledge our sins, he is faithful and just and will forgive our sins and cleanse us from every wrongdoing. If we say, "We have not sinned," we make him a liar, and his word is not in us.

The next one on the St. Michael card reads and summons him to the side of her children in the agony of death.

Prayer For Those in Agony

O St. Joseph, protector of those in agony, take pity on those who at this very moment when I pray to thee are engaged in their last combat.

O blessed Joseph, take pity on my soul too when the hour of the final battle shall arrive for me. Then, O my holy patron, do not abandon me, but grant me thine assistance; show that thou art my good father, and obtain that my Divine Savior may receive me with mercy into that abode where the elect enjoy a life that shall never end. Amen.

Jesus, Mary and Joseph (loved one), I give Thee my heart and my soul.
Jesus, Mary and Joseph, assist "name" in their last agony.
Jesus, Mary and Joseph, breathe forth their soul in peace with thee. Amen.
Eternal Father we pray for the souls in the Agony of Death. Amen.

St. Michael - Angel of Purgatory

How long do souls remain in Purgatory?

Purgatory will only exit until the final judgement. After a soul is judged during the final judgement, all just souls will go to Heaven, while all others will be sent to hell. Purgatory will no longer exist after the final judgement. Scripture says that nothing unclean can enter heaven.

Purgatory is the state of those who die in God's friendship, assured of their eternal salvation, but who still have need of purification to enter into the happiness of heaven.

Is Purgatory in the Bible?

You can find Purgatory in 1 Corinthians 3:9, 17 reads,

For we are God's co-workers; you are God's field, God's building.

According to the grace of God given to me, like a wise master builder I laid a foundation, and another is building upon it. But each one must be care how he builds upon it, for no one can lay a foundation other than the one that is there, namely, Jesus Christ. If anyone builds on this foundation with gold, silver, precious stones, wood, hay, or straw, the work of each will come to light, for the Day will disclose it. IT will be revealed with fire, and the fire itself will test the quality of each one's work. If the work stands that someone built upon the foundation, that person will receive a wage. But if someone's work is burned up, that one will suffer loss; the person will be saved, but only as through fire. Do you not know that you are the temple of God, and that the Spirit of God dwells in you? If anyone destroys God's temple, God will destroy that person; for the temple of God, which you are, is holy.

Judas praying for bodies who had fallen in battle and may have died in sin. A purgatory prayer, in 2 Maccabees 12:38, 46 reads; Judas rallied his army and went to the city of Adullam. As the seventh day was approaching, they purified themselves according to custom and kept the Sabbath there. On the following day, since the task had now become urgent, Judas and his companions went to gather up the bodies of the fallen and bury them with their kindred in their ancestral tombs. But under the tunic of each of the dead they found amulets sacred to the idols of Jamnia, which the law forbids the Jews to wear. So it was clear to all that this was why these men had fallen. They all therefore praised the ways of the Lord, the just judge who brings to light the things that are hidden. Turning to supplication, they prayed that the sinful deed might be fully blotted out. The noble Judas exhorted the people to keep themselves free from sin, for they had seen with their own eyes what had happened because of the sin of those who had fallen. He then took up a collection among all his soldiers, amounting to two thousand silver drachmas, which he sent to Jerusalem to provide for an expiatory sacrifice. In doing this he acting in a very excellent and noble way, inasmuch as he had the resurrection in mind; for if he were not expecting the fallen to rise again, it would have been superfluous and foolish to pray for the dead. But if he did this with a view to the splendid reward that await those who had gone to rest in godliness, it was a holy and pious thought. Thus he made atonement for the dead that they might be absolved from their sin.

Lastly, when the end time is here it is Jesus Christ, St Michael and God Almighty who will unfurl once more the standard of the cross and sound the last trumpet.

1 Thessalonians 4:16, 17 reads:

For the Lord himself, with a word of command, with the voice of an archangel and with the trumpet of God, will come down from heaven, and the dead in Christ will rise first. Then we who are alive, who are left, will be caught up together with them in the clouds to meet the Lord in the air. Thus we shall always be with the Lord.

Revelation 19:20 reads: The beast was caught and with it the false prophet who had performed in its sight the signs by which he led astray those who had accepted the mark fo the beast and those who had worshiped its image. The two were thrown alive into the fiery pool burning with sulfur.

CHAPTER 11

Acknowledgements

To Immaculate Conception Church. The Jesuit Downtown Parish of Albuquerque N.M.

Fr. Warren Broussard, S.J. Pastor

Fr. Broussard, a member of the Central and Southern Province, was born in Lake Charles, Louisiana. He studied Theology at Regis College, the Jesuit School of Theology in Toronto, Canada and was ordained a priest in June 1988.

Our Deacons and Jesuits Community. Also St. Mary's Catholic School.

Fr. Warren Broussard sends out his Easter Greetings from Immaculate Conception in Downtown Albuquerque, N.M. Watch and share, Rev. Broussard YouTube video.

The Jesuits

We are the Society of Jesus, a Roman Catholic order of priests and brothers founded half a millennium ago by the soldier who turned his life to Christianity, Ignatius Loyola. But most people call us the Jesuits.

In the vision of our founder, we seek to "Find God in all things." We dedicate ourselves to the, "Greater Glory of God" and the good of all humanity. And we do so gratefully in collaboration with others who share our values, including lay persons. They have become part of the "we," the extended Jesuit family.

With 16,000-plus priests, brothers, scholastics and novices worldwide, we are the largest male religious order in the Catholic Church. We are pastors, teachers, and chaplains. We are also doctors, lawyers, and astronomers, among many other roles in church and society. In our varied ministries, we care for the whole person; body, mind, and soul. And especially in our education ministries, we seek to nurture "men and women for others."

Jesuits draw on the rich tradition of Ignatian spirituality and reflection. In our retreat centers, campus ministries, and other setting, we offer these resources to all who want to discern God's presence in their lives. At the same time, we also aim to be "contemplatives in action, people who bring this spirituality into the wide world. That includes our work on behalf of global justice, peace, and the the Glory of God Almighty, Jesus Christ our Saviors. And all the angels in Heaven Amen.

Immaculate Conception Church

Does the term Immaculate Conception describe Mary's Conception of Jesus?

What is the Conception of Jesus called?

Immaculate Conception, Roman Catholic dogma asserting that Mary, the mother of Jesus, was preserved free from the effects of the sin of Adam (usually referred to as original sin) from the first instant of her conception.

Luke 1:26, 35, In the sixth month, the angel Gabriel was sent from God to a town of Galilee called Nazareth, to a virgin betrothed to a man named Joseph, and the virgin's name was Mary. And coming to her, he said, "Hail, favored one! The Lord is with you." But she was greatly troubled at what was said and pondered what sort of greeting this might be. Then the angel said to her, "Do not be afraid, Mary, for you have found favor with God. Behold, you will conceive in your womb and bear a son, and you shall name him Jesus. He will be great and will be called Son of the Most High, and the Lord God will give him the throne of David his father, and he will rule over the house of Jacob forever, and of his kingdom there will be no end. But Mary said to the angel, "How can this be, since I have no relations with a man?" And the angel said to her in reply, "The holy Spirit will come upon you, and the power of the Most High will overshadow you. Therefore the child to be born will be called holy, the Son of God. And behold, Elizabeth, your relative, has also conceived a son in her old age, and this is the sixth month for her who was called barren; for nothing will be impossible for God." Mary said, "Behold, I am the handmaid of the Lord. May it be done to me according to your word." Then the angel departed from her.

A thankful letter to say thank you Paster Fr. Warren Broussard and all the Deacons and Jesuits, and to our St. Mary's Catholic School.

I, John M. Gurule, was very humbled and grateful to be of service to you Father Broussard and the Immaculate Conception Church.

Thank you for all your hard work and the best preaching I ever heard. Your Jesuit brothers in Jesus Christ thank you all.

Who is Bishop Byron Rogers and lovely wife Selma Rogers? Both are church leaders, they both lead an individual congregation.

Powerhouse was founded by Bishop Byron Rogers in 1994, after serving as Senior Pastor for 18 years. Bishop Rogers along with his lovely wife Selma Rogers Retired in September 2012.

First and foremost, Powerhouse a Church of God is a determinedly Christian Church. It is built upon the person of Jesus Christ, the Son of God, the doctrines and practices of the church are based upon His teaching.

Pentecostal Church

In 1896, many members of the church of God, experienced a spiritual outpouring they identified as the baptism of the holy spirit. Because it was similar to the experience of the early Christians on the day of Pentecost, it came to be called a Pentecostal experience, an enrichment of the Christian life through the power of the holy spirit that empowered believers to be effective witnesses of Christ; The principle distinctive of the church as a Pentecostal organization is its belief in speaking with other tongues as the spirit give the utterance. Utterance definition, voicing, saying, speaking, expression, delivery, and sounding aloud.

An Evangelistic Church

From its inception our church and those affiliated with the larger church of God has been a revival movement, Evangelism has been in the forefront of all its activated. The church has maintained an aggressive effort to take the message of Christ throughout the world by all means and methods. Every program of the church reflects an evangelistic attitude: revivalism, conferences, worship services, teaching, preaching and its missionary efforts.

I met Bishop Rogers from another Pastor Beraldo Romero, a friend of mine.

I went to Pastor Beraldo and Lucy Church for years, Agape Faith Ministries. Beraldo and his wife Lucy Romero retired also. So I stayed at the Powerhouse Ministries and I've been working with Byron Rogers for 15 years.

By working and going to the Powerhouse Church, I've built up my own spiritualty, along with a friendship with Bishop Roger and his family.

I want to thank you Bishop Rogers and your family for all your help. I've learned a lot and still learning from you Sir Rogers, Blessing, Blessing, Blessing to you and your family. May God Bless your life. John M Gurule.

Matthew 7:13, 14

I, John Michael Gurule, acknowledge that we have to walk the narrow way to eternal life, never ending life in Heaven where my family is.

Son - Michael Ray Gurule - Jessica Little Michael - Little Jessica.

Cindy Romero - from Cincinnati, September 2015-2019 - passed from cancer.

Prayer to St. Raphael - Healing, Deliverance, Protection, Peace, Prosperity, Happy Unions, Purity.

Marriage and Healing of Sarah, Expulsion of the Demon.

St Raphael and Tobiah's return Journey to Neneveh and The healing of Tobit. Read the book of Tobit, God Almighty sent St. Raphael to these two families.

I, John Michael Gurule, will write about part of the book of Tobit.

Tobit chapter 6:14, 18, But Tobiah said to Raphael in reply, "Brother Azariah, I have heard that she has already been given in marriage to seven husbands, and that they have died in the bridal chamber. On the very night they approached her, they would die. I have also heard it said that it was a demon that killed them. So now I too am afraid of this demon, because it is in love with her and does not harm her; but it kills any man who wishes to come to her. I am my father's only child. If I should die, I would bring the life of my father and mother down to their grave in sorrow over me; they have no other son to bury them!

Raphael said to him; "Do you not remember your father's commands? He ordered you to marry a woman from your own ancestral family. Now listen to me, brother; do not worry about that demon. Take Sarah. I know that tonight she will be given to you as your wife! When you go into the bridal chamber, take some of the fish's liver and the heart, and place them on the embers intended for incense, and an odor will be given off. As soon as the demon smells the odor, it will flee and never again show itself near her. Then when you are about to have intercourse with her, both of you must first get up to pray. Beg the Lord of heaven that mercy and protection be granted you. Do not be afraid, for she was set apart for you before the world existed. You will save her, and she will go with you. And I assume that you will have children by her, and they will be like brothers for you, so do not worry.

When Tobiah heard Raphael's words that she was his kinswoman, and of the lineage of his ancestral house, he loved her deeply, and his heart was truly set on her.

Marriage and Healing of Sarah, Tobit Chapter 7: 1,17,

When they entered Ecbatana, Tobiah said, "Brother Azariah, bring me straight to the house of our kinsman Raguel." So he did, and they came to the house of Raguel, whom they found seated by his courtyard gate. They greeted him first, and he answered, "Many greeting to you, brothers! Welcome! You have come in peace! Now enter in peace!" Now enter in peace! And he brought them into his house. He said to his wife Edna, "How this young man resembles Tobit, the son of my uncle!" So Edna asked them, saying, "Where are you from, brothers?" They answered, "We are descendants of Naphtali, now captives in Nineveh." She said to them, "Do you know our kinsman Tobit?" They answered her, "Indeed, we do know him!" She asked, "Is he well?" They answered, "Yes, he is alive and well." Then Tobiah said, "He is my father!" Raguel jumped up, kissed him, and broke into tears. Then, finding words, he said, A blessing upon you, son! You are the son of a good and noble father. What a terrible misfortune that a man so righteous and charitable has been afflicted with blindness!" He embraced his kinsman Tobiah and continued to weep. His wife Edna also wept for Tobit; and their daughter Sarah also began to weep.

First is the marriage of Tobiah and Sarah. Afterward, Raguel slaughtered a ram from the flock and gave them a warm reception. When they had washed, bathed, and reclined to eat and drink, Tobiah said to Raphael, "Brother Azariah, ask Raguel to give me my kinswoman Sarah." Raguel overheard the words; so he said to the young man: "Eat and drink and be merry tonight, for no man has a greater right to marry my daughter Sarah than you, brother. Besides, not even I have the right to give her to anyone but you, because you are my closest relative. However, son, I must frankly tell you the truth. I have given her in marriage to seven husbands who were kinsmen of ours, and all died on the very night they approached her. But now, son, eat and drink. The Lord will look after you both." Tobiah answered, "I will neither eat nor drink anything here until you settle what concerns me."

Raguel said to him: "I will do it. She is yours as decreed by the Book of Moses. It has been decided in heaven that she be given to you! Take your kinswoman; from now on you are her brother, and she is your sister. She is given to you today and here ever after. May the Lord of heaven prosper you both tonight, son and grant you mercy and peace." Then Raguel called his daughter Sarah, and she came to him. He took her by the hand and gave her to Tobiah with these words: "Take her according to the law. According to the decree written in the Book of Moses I give her to be your wife. Take her and bring her safely to your father. And may the God of heaven grant both of you a safe journey in peace!" He then called her mother and told her to bring writing materials. He wrote out a copy of a marriage contract stating that he gave Sarah to Tobiah as his wife as decreed by the law of Moses. Her mother brought the material, and he drew up the contract, to which he affixed his seal. Afterward they began to eat and drink. Later Raguel called his wife Edna and said, "My sister, prepare the other bedroom and bring Sarah there. She went, made the bed in the room, as he had told her, and brought Sarah there. After she had cried over her, she wiped away her tears and said, "Take courage, my daughter! May the Lord of heaven grant you joy in place of your grief! Courage, my daughter!" Then she left.

Tobit 8:1, 5,

Expulsion of the Demon. Expulsion is defined as forcing someone to leave or forcing something out of the body.

When they had finished eating and drinking, they wanted to retire. So they brought the young man out and led him to the bedroom. Tobiah, mindful of Raphael's instructions, took the fish's liver and heart from the bag where he had them, and put them on the embers intended for incense. The odor of the fish repulsed the demon, and it fled to the upper regions of Egypt; Raphael went in pursuit of it and there bound it hand and foot. Then Raphael returned immediately.

When Sarah's parents left the bedroom and closed the door behind them, Tobiah rose from bed and said to his wife, "My sister, come, let us pray and beg our Lord to grant us mercy and protection." She got up, and they started to pray and beg that they might be protected. He began with these words:

"Blessed are you, O God of our ancestors; blessed be your name forever and ever! Let the heavens and all your creation bless you forever."

Tobit 11:9, 18, Tobit's Sight Restored.

Then Anna ran up to her son, embraced him, and said to him, "Now that I have seen you again, son, I am ready to die!" And she sobbed aloud. Tobit got up and stumbled out through the courtyard gate to meet his son. Tobiah went up to him with the fish gall in his hand and blew into his eyes. Holding him firmly, he said, "Courage, father." Then he applied the medicine to his eyes, and it made them sting. Tobiah used both hands to peel the white scales from the corners of his eyes. Tobit saw his son and threw his arms around him. Weeping, he exclaimed, "I can see you, son, the light of my eyes!" Then he prayed,

Blessed be God,
    blessed be his great name,
    and blessed be all his holy angels.
May his great name be with us,
    and blessed be all the angels
    throughout all the ages.
God it was who afflicted me,
    and God who has had mercy on me.
    Now I see my son Tobiah!

Then Tobit went back in, rejoicing and praising God with full voice. Tobiah related to his father how his journey had been a success, that he had brought back the money; and that he had married Raguel's daughter Sarah, who was about to arrive, for she was near the gate of Nineveh.

Rejoicing and blessing God, Tobit went out to the gate of Nineveh to meet his daughter-in-law. When the people of Nineveh saw him coming, walking along briskly, with no one leading him by the hand, they were amazed. Before them all Tobit proclaimed how God had shown mercy to him and opened his eyes. When Tobit came up to Sarah, the wife of his son Tobiah, he blessed her and said: "Welcome, my daughter! Blessed be your God for bringing you to us, daughter! Blessed are your father and your mother. Blessed be my son Tobiah, and blessed be you, daughter! Welcome to your home with blessing and joy. Come in daughter!" That day there was joy for all the Jews who lived in Nineveh. Ahiqar and his nephew Nadin were also on hand to rejoice with Tobit. Tobiah's wedding feast was celebrated with joy for seven days, and many gifts were given to him.

St. Raphael wages, Tobit 12: 1,5,

When the wedding celebration came to an end, Tobit called his son Tobiah and said to him. "Son see to it that you pay his wages to the man who made the journey with you and give him a bonus too." Tobiah said: "Father, how much shall I pay him? It would not hurt to give him half the wealth he brought back with me. He led me back safe and sound, healed my wife, brought the money back with me, and healed you. How much should I pay him?" Tobit answered, "It is only fair, son, that he should receive half of all that he brought back." So Tobiah called Raphael and said, "Take as your wages half of all that you have brought back, and farewell!"

Exhortation, strongly exhorting people, and the followers of Jesus Christ to do the right thing in the Lord. Urging and encouragement to all Christians. Tobit 12:6, 10 read:

Raphael called the two of them side privately and said to them: "Bless God and give him thanks before all the living for the good things he has done for you, by blessing and extolling his name in song. To praise highly, and to glorify the name of the Lord. To Proclaim before all with due honor the deeds of God, and do not be slack in thanking him. A king's secret should be kept secret, but one must declare the works of God and give thanks with due honor. Do good, and evil will not overtake you. Prayer with fasting is good. Almsgiving with righteousness is better than wealth with wickedness. It is better to give alms than to store up gold, for almsgiving saves from death, and purges all sin. Those who give alms will enjoy a full life, but those who commit sin and do evil are their own worst enemies."

St. Raphael's Identity, Tobit 12:11, 15,

"I shall now tell you the whole truth and conceal nothing at all from you. I have already said to you, 'A king's secret should be kept secret, but one must declare the works of God with due honor.' Now when you, Tobit, and Sarah prayed, it was I who presented the record of your prayer before the Glory of the Lord; and likewise whenever you used to bury the dead. When you did not hesitate to get up and leave your dinner in order to go and bury the dead man, I was sent to put you to the test. At the same time, however, God sent me to heal you and your daughter-in-law Sarah. I am Raphael, one of the seven angels who stand and serve before the Glory of the Lord.

Greatly shaken, the two of them fell prostrate in fear. But Raphael said to them: "Do not fear; peace be with you! Bless God now and forever. As for me. When I was with you, I was not acting out of any favor on my part, but by God's will. So bless God every day; give praise with song. Even though you saw me eat and drink, I did not eat or drink anything; what you were seeing was a vision. So now bless the Lord on earth and give thanks to God. Look, I am ascending to the one who sent me. Write down all that has happened to you." And he ascended. They stood up but were no longer able to see him. They kept blessing God and singing his praises, and they continued to give thanks for these marvelous works that God had done, because an angel of God appeared to them. This is the St. Raphael one of the seven angels speaking.

When we pray, God sends us angels, we think of Jesus, Mary, and an angel who brought good news. Also we think of the prayer Zechariah, the father of John the Baptist, who preached repentances. Jesus and John the Baptist were when Zechariah prayed, God gave him good news by sending the angel Gabriel. Again with the prophet Daniel prayed and God sent Gabriel an angel from heaven. This next story is about Rachael Padilla who was in a bad accident, she also prayed to God Almighty for help, an angel appears to her. This is Rachael's story.

Rachael Padilla, her testimony is evidence or proof provided by the existence or an appearance, in this case an angel of the Lord.

This is Rachael's Testimony.

This incident happened on April 29, 2014. It was my friend's birthday on April the 30th, so I wanted to walk to Smiths to get her a cake. I was walking by the bus station, and I see a car at the stop sign. They waved at me to walk past, so I did, and as I was almost to the sidewalk a car came so fast and hit me. As all this happened, I was wearing basketball shorts and my shorts got connected to the car, I got dragged by the car 200 ft. I was screaming at the people to stop, and they just went faster, to try to get me to fall off. They got really close to the cars parked on the side of the street, so I knew I had to push myself off the car, as I pushed myself off the car I did a complete backflip and landed on my head, that's when I realized I had a huge, huge knot on my head. It was gushing blood. I looked at my arms and legs and I had 3rd degree road rash burns all over my body. I had a shattered knee, so the Dr. said there was no way I could have got up and ran home. All I remember after this was I felt something which I believe was an angel picked me up and help me run home. My mom rushed me to the hospital, where we found out I had a broken wrist, and a shattered knee, 3rd degree road rash burns and a severe concussion. Thank God I didn't have a brain bleed because it was a huge possibility. The Doctor said I was lucky to be alive. As I was in the hospital they had to scrub all the rock out of my skin with a little brush. It hurt so bad and they said my skin will never be the same. That is why I got tattoos because I'm still very insecure about the color of my skin. After the incident we found out it was a drunk driver. I had to use crutches for a long time, I had a cast and a lot of bandages for a very long time, the healing process was so rough I couldn't sleep at all. I truly thank God every day for helping me, because I know if the Angel didn't pick me up that night, I wouldn't be alive to tell you this story. I learned a lot about Jesus from John Michael Gurule. He has taught me, and showed me that anything is possible with God, and just a simple prayer. He's a wonderful man and has taught me a lot about the Lord. I read John's 1st book "A Forty Year Journey with God in Albuquerque N.M." and I learned a lot from the book. One of the main things I learned is as long as you believe, anything is possible. John has been sober now for over 3 years and he has completely turned himself around. When I first met John, it was at a bus stop on San Mateo and Central, where I was headed to work at the library and the bus was running late. He was riding a bike and was headed to watch a movie. He gave me his card and I texted him. He was living in a camper at his sister's place. Fast forward to December 2020, John is the hardest working man I know. He never gives up. He will continue to try and try until he succeeds. He now has his own place, he has a truck, trailer, and tools. He is disabled also, he got ran over by a city dump truck, and crushed his right foot. As to back when he didn't have anything at all. John is a wonderful man and has taught me so much about Jesus. I have never done drugs or alcohol, because I saw a couple of people I know, lose absolutely everything even their own children because of drugs and alcohol. I hate seeing people struggle especially if its someone close to me. John has talked to me about his second book. He has worked hard all year on this book. He had a goal of finishing it by the end of 2020 and he did it. I'm so proud of him. I do understand that God is with us at all times. I pray to him meaning God every day and night and thank him for everything he has done for me. John has given me my first Catholic bible. I plan to read it and I do enjoy hearing John preach. I know he knows what he is saying, I have looked in the bible and what he is saying is true.

I really do appreciate and am thankful that God has brought John Michael Gurule into my life. He has shown me so much these past 3 years. He's a wonderful and blessed man. He prays so much and I'm grateful, I have someone that can show me all about Jesus and God.

Thank you John.
This is my Testimony.
Rachael Padilla

A story of heaven and Hell. Luke 16:14, The Pharisees, who were loved money, heard all these things, and sneered Him.

Luke 16:19, 3, There was a rich man who dressed in purple garments and fine linen and dined sumptuously each day. And lying at his door was a poor man named Lazarus, covered with sores, who would gladly have eaten his fill of the scraps that fell from the rich man's table. Dogs even used to come and lick his sores. When the poor man died, he was carried away by angels to the bosom of Abraham. The rich man also died and was buried, and from the netherworld where he was in torment, he raised his eyes and saw Abraham far off and Lazarus at his side. And he cried out, 'Father Abraham, have pity on me. Send Lazarus to dip the tip of his finger in water and cool my tongue, for I am suffering torment in these flames.' Abraham replied, 'My child, remember that you received what was good during your lifetime while Lazarus likewise received what was bad; but now he is comforted here, whereas you are tormented. Moreover, between us and you a great chasm is established to prevent anyone from crossing who might wish to go from our side to yours or from your side to ours.' He said, 'Then I beg you, father, send him to my father's house, for I have five brothers, so that he may warn them, lest they too come to this place of torment.' But Abraham replied, 'They have Moses and the prophets. Let them listen to them.' He said, 'Oh no, father Abraham, but if someone from the dead goes to them, they will repent.' Then Abraham said, 'If they will not listen to Moses and the prophets, neither will they be persuaded if someone should rise from the dead.'

The bible I used to write these scriptures in this book is the American Bible Society.

Fr. Warren Broussard and John Gurule

Bishop and Selma Rogers

Rachael Padilla

Rachael Padilla

John Gurule

Rachael Padilla and John Gurule

Lightning Source UK Ltd.
Milton Keynes UK
UKHW012048110621
385375UK00007B/559/J